A People of Grace

Becoming
Disciples
Together

OF

SAM BARBER

f

THE FOUNDRY
PUBLISHING

The Foundry Publishing®
PO Box 419527
Kansas City, MO 64141
thefoundrypublishing.com

ISBN 978-0-8341-4182-7

Printed in the
United States of America

Cover design: Caines Design
Interior design: Sharon Page

Library of Congress Cataloging-in-Publication Data
A complete catalog record for this book is available from the Library of Congress.

10 9 8 7 6 5 4 3 2 1

CONTENTS

INTRODUCTION

On September 12, 1962, President John F. Kennedy stood at the podium of Rice University and announced that the United States would put a person on the moon within ten years. From our technologically advanced vantage point today we shudder at the audacity of that vision. However, on July 20, 1969, Neil Armstrong became the first human to set foot on the moon. His words, "That's one small step for [a] man; one giant leap for mankind,"[1] resounded across the crackling radio both profound and prophetic.

Kennedy's vision and Neil Armstrong's footsteps dominate the history books, but like most major accomplishments, a closer look reveals that we should acknowledge more than just the exploits of two men. The British Broadcasting Corporation (BBC) recently produced a series of articles highlighting the Apollo space program. The BBC's conservative estimates

---

1. "One Small Step," Apollo 11 Lunar Surface Journal, accessed September 19, 2022, https://history.nasa.gov/alsj/a11/a11.step.html.

indicate that the successful Apollo 11 mission to the moon and back required the combined efforts of over 400,000 people!

Many of us celebrate the work of Margot Lee Shetterly in her book *Hidden Figures*, where she brings to light the enormous contribution of a group of African American women known as the West Computers. The recent film named after the book does a marvelous job of demonstrating the value of these heroic women and the significant impact they had on NASA, the Apollo 11 mission, and the fight for gender and racial equality. The West Computers were an essential fraction of the 400,000 contributors to the Apollo 11 mission.

The remarkable and historic work of these many contributors illustrates a powerful truth that anchors this book. Significant things, the kinds of things that test the limits of human capabilities and change the world, are seldom solo endeavors. We may remember Kennedy's audacious vision or Armstrong's first steps on the moon, but the successful journey to the moon and safely back to earth would not have been possible without the cooperative efforts of 399,998 other people dedicated to a common cause and working together to see it become reality.

There really is strength in numbers, and the Bible agrees. There may be things in the Scriptures that seem a bit out of reach for our finite minds, but nothing could be clearer than Jesus's words to his disciples before he ascended into heaven: "All authority in heaven and on earth has been given to me. Therefore go and make disciples of all nations, baptizing them in the name of the Father and of the Son and of the Holy Spirit, and teaching them to obey everything I have commanded you.

And surely I am with you always, to the very end of the age"
(Matt. 28:18-20).

The call of Christ to be and make disciples is straightforward and clear. However, many well-meaning believers struggle to make it a reality in their own lives. We don't struggle to understand Jesus, but we do struggle to carry out his call.

What if our approach to Jesus's commission has had a fatal flaw? What if our very best efforts to discipline ourselves and disciple effectively fail because we overlook something obvious in the ministry of Jesus? What if we took a cue from a powerful movement in our "get healthy" culture and reapplied that cue to our discipleship ministries?

Have I piqued your interest? What could possibly be so obvious yet overlooked in our discipleship efforts? I'll give you a hint from Apollo 11: if you want to go to the moon, you'll never get there alone. That is, if you want to do something significant, something that might change the world, something that is really difficult to do, you'll never accomplish it by yourself. These kinds of achievements only come when we approach them *together*.

Sadly, too often we approach our spiritual journey as a solo endeavor when Jesus taught us to live in community and to pursue his will as a team effort. Jesus taught us a particular way to be together, and John Wesley, seventeen hundred years later, effectively systematized it for the people of his time. What Wesley did then, we can adapt today. Jesus modeled discipleship for us and then handed us the responsibility to carry on his work. Wouldn't it be wonderful to see the church come together around that purpose, take up Jesus's example, and fulfill the Great Commission? Perhaps the next great move of God in the world will arise from people who embody this vision.

If you want to go to the moon, you'll never get there alone. If you want to be a disciple and make disciples, you can't do that alone either. Let's discover together an innovative and effective method for discipleship.

one
THE REACH OF GRACE
For God So Loved

Augustine of Hippo (AD 354–430) wasn't always a saint. Though reared as a Christian by a believing mother, he chose not to follow Jesus in his early years, even fathering a child by a woman with whom he had a long-standing relationship. Augustine went on to become well educated and a prominent teacher of rhetoric, but his life lacked a deeper meaning. Eventually, Augustine experienced the saving grace of God and was baptized. He then took up the monastic life and became a bishop in the church. A prolific writer, in his best-known work, his spiritual autobiography, *Confessions*, he makes this powerful statement: "Thou hast made us for thyself, O Lord, and our heart is restless until it finds its rest in thee."[1]

---

1. Augustine, *Confessions*, 1.1.1.

Augustine's quote describes the restlessness of people in every age. To be human is to be painfully aware of a sense of incompleteness. We each have a gnawing suspicion that something isn't quite right deep within us. In time we begin to search for something to satisfy what is missing in us. Clara Tear Williams, who penned the following words, preserved a haunting description of the inner conflict in Augustine and in each of us:

> All my life-long I had panted
> For a drink from some cool spring
> That I hoped would quench the burning
> Of the thirst I felt within.
>
> Feeding on the husks around me
> Till my strength was almost gone,
> Longed my soul for something better,
> Only still to hunger on.
>
> Poor I was, and sought for riches,
> Something that would satisfy;
> But the dust I gathered round me
> Only mocked my soul's sad cry.[2]

It doesn't take much effort to examine the culture around us or even our own biographies to realize that the search for meaning and satisfaction in life is a universal quest, and anything but the redeeming presence of Christ is unfulfilling.

---

2. Clara Tear Williams, "Satisfied," in *Sing to the Lord* (Kansas City: Lillenas, 1993), no. 383.

What is the answer to this intrinsic ache? We find this answer in Jesus, who is the way, truth, and life, but how can we find him? Perhaps just as important is the question, What should life be about once we become followers of Jesus? How can we so pattern our lives after Jesus that we don't miss out on his plans for us? This book attempts to answer these questions in the following ways:

- We begin by exploring the amazing grace of God. We discuss the ways that God has chosen to bring his presence into our lives.

- We continue by defining the purpose of all God's grace. That is, we examine why God would go to such extraordinary lengths to redeem us.

- Once we discover God's intention for our lives, we learn not only how to stay in step with God but also how to engage with God in God's redemptive plans in the world.

- Finally, we learn a specific method of discipleship that keeps us growing so that the purpose we long for and the purposes of God are aligned. There is no better life than a life lived in harmony with God.

The good news is that just as John Newton's classic song "Amazing Grace" affirms, God does indeed offer us amazing grace. God is seeking you and has been your whole life. In fact, God is seeking every person. When we understand God's grace and God's mission and pursue it together, the renewal of the church becomes a reality.

Juan Valdez and Prevenient Grace

In 1958, the National Federation of Coffee Growers of Colombia enlisted the help of an advertising firm to create a campaign that would highlight the characteristics of genuine Colombian coffee. The firm created the fictional character Juan Valdez and his faithful mule, Conchita. Juan Valdez represented the hardworking Colombian coffee farmer whose diligence ensured the best-tasting coffee in the world.

The ad campaign worked. By the time the early 1970s rolled around, the Juan Valdez character was well established in American pop culture. His iconic image eventually came to stand for virtually all coffee in American advertising.

Television programs were often punctuated with commercials featuring the gentle Colombian farmer. In one commercial, Conchita the mule, standing at a bedside early in the morning, nuzzles a man awake. Then, just as the man finds his glasses, Conchita disappears. The man's wife, awakened by the commotion, stumbles to the pantry to start her day and is greeted by Juan Valdez, who hands her a can of Colombian coffee with a cheery, "Buenos días." Later, the husband spots Juan and Conchita on the subway speeding away. The message was clear: Juan Valdez and his coffee were everywhere, and everyone's life would be improved by accepting the gift of coffee from the gentle Colombian farmer.

As we consider the grace of God, the character of Juan Valdez is a helpful illustration. Like Juan Valdez, God is everywhere. No matter where we find ourselves, God is there. When

Everyone's life would
be blessed by accepting
the grace offered by the
humble Savior, and Jesus
is miraculously present
everywhere we turn.

○ ○ ○

we are waking up, going throughout our day, busy at work, or relaxing at home, God is present, offering grace.

Also, consider how much the gentle farmer's demeanor resembles Jesus. There was no marketing "sizzle" with Juan Valdez, just the embodiment of faithfulness and goodness. Now picture the gentle Savior showing up in virtually every area of our lives, humbly and kindly offering us, not a can of coffee, but his love and mercy. The message about coffee is even more powerful in Jesus. Everyone's life would be blessed by accepting the grace offered by the humble Savior, and Jesus is miraculously present everywhere we turn.

Theologians call this expression of God's grace *prevenient*. Prevenient grace is the grace that goes before any decision on our part to choose to follow Jesus. Prevenient grace is the ongoing activity of our faithful God, drawing people to himself. This expression of God's grace is essential because without God's grace, we are powerless to choose him. So great is the depth of our depravity, so tight the grip of sin on the human heart, that without the intervening grace of God, we are unable to choose the way of God.

A certain man, in his testimony, was reflecting on his decision to follow Jesus and began to describe God's persistence. He said that no matter how hard he tried to avoid thinking about God or sensing God's presence, it seemed that God was constantly present. This experience is echoed in Psalm 139:

Where can I go from your Spirit?
Where can I flee from your presence?
If I go up to the heavens, you are there;
    if I make my bed in the depths, you are there.

If I rise on the wings of the dawn,

    if I settle on the far side of the sea,

even there your hand will guide me,

    your right hand will hold me fast. (Vv. 7-10)

The man said he broke down and begged God to leave him alone, and God would not. In time, the persistent prevenient grace of God was more than the man could resist, and in a moment of surrender, he offered himself to God, receiving forgiveness of sins and a new lease on life.

Prevenient grace means that God is everywhere and is continuously drawing us and reaching out for us. How remarkable is the extent to which God is willing to go to get our attention and draw us into a saving relationship!

God's prevenient grace is at work right now in the heart and life of every person. Prevenient grace reached us, and prevenient grace is reaching out to those for whom we are praying—the wayward family member, the coworker or classmate, the stranger across the restaurant. How encouraging to know that our faithful God never ceases to draw people toward a saving relationship. The collective strength of NASA in the 1960s put a man on the moon. Imagine the impact of the people of God transformed by his grace!

Prevenient grace goes before any decision to follow Jesus. God continuously reaches out to us, calling us to himself. The goal of prevenient grace is our acceptance of Jesus as Savior and Lord, and it is here that we experience saving grace.

The Man in a Hole and Saving Grace

In the ever-popular television series *The West Wing*, chief of staff Leo McGarry shares a story with another cabinet member, Josh Lyman, who is battling post-traumatic stress after being shot in an attempt on the president's life. The story is about a guy who falls into a hole that he cannot climb out. He cries out to a doctor and a priest, who go on their way after doing little to help. Finally, a friend shows up and, on hearing the guy's cry for help, jumps in the hole. The guy responds, "'Are you stupid? Now we're both down here!' The friend says, 'Yeah, but I've been down here before, and I know the way out.'"[3]

We all need a friend like that; someone who will come right to where we are during our darkest moments and help us. But actually we all do have a friend just like that. Can we recognize God's saving grace highlighted in this anecdote?

Consider our reality, according to Scripture: "Therefore, just as sin entered the world through one man, and death through sin, . . . in this way death came to all people, because all sinned" (Rom. 5:12).

As adorable as we were as babies, as precious as we were as children, and as winsome as we are in adulthood, we all came into this world with a sinful nature. Our hearts come pre-wired for selfishness. Thanks to the fall of humanity detailed in Genesis 3, our "operating system" is designed to facilitate our

---

3. Quoted at IMDb.com, https://www.imdb.com/title/tt0745664/characters /nm0817983, from *The West Wing*, season 2, episode 10, "Noël," directed by Thomas Schlamme, aired December 20, 2000, on NBC.

wants and desires even when they undervalue the wants and desires of God and others.

Paul the apostle puts a finer point on the human condition when he writes, "And you were dead in the trespasses and sins in which you once walked, following the course of this world, following the prince of the power of the air, the spirit that is now at work in the sons of disobedience—among whom we all once lived in the passions of our flesh, carrying out the desires of the body and the mind, and were by nature children of wrath, like the rest of mankind" (Eph. 2:1-3, ESV).

Our plight is grim indeed, but we must consider the saving grace of our loving God: "For God so loved the world that he gave his one and only Son, that whoever believes in him shall not perish but have eternal life. For God did not send his Son into the world to condemn the world, but to save the world through him" (John 3:16-17).

Our loving God has made a remedy for sin through the gracious gift of his Son, Jesus. It is by believing in Jesus as Savior and receiving the gift of grace by faith that we are saved.

Let's reimagine the story of God with McGarry's tale as a backdrop. The impact of the fall of humanity in Genesis 3 means that every person, regardless of era or pedigree, enters this world under the weight of sin. This sinful predisposition means that we act out in sinful ways. We have all witnessed a toddler's temper tantrum and occasionally the grown-up version of an angry meltdown. Perhaps we've experienced temptation and failed to resist. Maybe we've harbored ill will in our hearts toward a person we perceive as a rival. Eighteenth-century pastor John Wesley helped us define this rebellion—this

○ ○ ○

Jesus has found us in a place we cannot escape on our own and has come to save us and to show us the way to new life.

○ ○ ○

sin—as a willful transgression against a known law of God. That is, we know what God has asked us to avoid, but we do it anyway. Similarly, we may know what God asks us to do, but we neglect to do it. It is our stubborn, self-centered will acting in opposition to God's best plans for us. It's the logical expression of a sinful nature.

Humanity has fallen in a hole, so to speak, and we can't get out. Despite our best human efforts, we discover that we are powerless to free ourselves from sin's grip. God, having created humanity for a much higher purpose than the struggle with sin, sent Jesus, who miraculously jumped down in the hole with us and invited us to follow him. Paul writes about Jesus to the Philippians, urging them to imitate Christ:

Who, being in very nature God,

did not consider equality with God something to be

used to his own advantage;

rather, he made himself nothing

by taking the very nature of a servant,

being made in human likeness.

And being found in appearance as a man,

he humbled himself

by becoming obedient to death—

even death on a cross! (Phil. 2:6-8)

When we were powerless to save ourselves, God sent his only Son, Jesus. It is through Jesus's exemplary life, death on the cross, and his bodily resurrection that the chains of sin are broken and we can be set free. Jesus's death atones for our sin, offering to us a clean slate through justification, a cosmic do-over in regeneration, and a new family in adoption as children of God.

Jesus knows the way out of the "hole." If we find comfort in McGarry's character saying "Yeah, but I've been down here before, and I know the way out," how much more comforting is it to remember that we, like the first disciples, hear Jesus saying, "Follow me"? Jesus has found us in a place we cannot escape on our own and has come to save us and to show us the way to new life.

What a powerful picture of saving grace! Long before we existed or understood our need for God, God went to extraordinary lengths to save us. God is a God of grace, and the Bible details his saving acts throughout history. The writer of Hebrews teaches us, "In the past God spoke to our ancestors through the prophets at many times and in various ways, but in these last days he has spoken to us by his Son, whom he appointed heir of all things, and through whom also he made the universe" (Heb. 1:1-2).

In Christ, God made our redemption possible. The saving grace of God reaches us in Christ, who finds us deep in our sin and offers us the way to new and eternal life. But as every believer knows, the forgiveness of sins is only part of the battle. Even after our salvation, there is a battle waging within us. The desire for God and the desire for self seem to be at odds. Is the salvation offered in Christ Jesus limited to the covering of our sins? Or is there a deeper work that God intends? This is where God's sanctifying grace comes into the picture.

Lucky the Discount Dog
and Sanctifying Grace

As with so many parents, we promised our four-year-old son a pet. After scouring the newspaper, my wife found a local veterinarian with an ad for a free dog. We would later learn that the concept of "free dog" is a myth. The ad should have said "discount dog," since we wound up investing quite a bit of money in our "free" dog. We made some phone calls, agreed to give this dog a home, purchased a collar and leash, and made our way to the vet's office. We signed a few papers, and they brought the dog out to us. She was a black Lab mix, but her coat was riddled with tiny wounds from a lifetime of fleas. She winced at our every move, unsure of whether to trust us. She had been abused and abandoned.

The vet offered a few comforting words about the dog's potential and assured us that she would soon warm to our affection. She was, frankly, pitiful. We arranged for the vet to keep her for a few more hours, went and picked up our son, and brought him to the vet's office. The technicians brought the dog out, and our son's face lit up with delight. He took to her immediately and was thrilled, despite her rugged appearance. As we loaded her in the car, I asked him what he wanted to name her. He barely paused before announcing, "Her name is Lucky."

For the first few weeks, Lucky was afraid. Every noise spooked her. She had several accidents in the house, and when we left her alone in the backyard, she jumped the fence and ran away. We would jump in the car and scour the neighborhood looking for her. Eventually we would find her, coax her into the car, and take her home. Evenings found us taking turns applying the medicine the vet had given us to her wounds and brushing out her coat. It seemed for a while that the arrangement wasn't going to work. She struggled to trust us. In time, however, Lucky learned what love was and decided that life in our little bungalow with a fenced yard was pretty good. She had all the affection she could want, a bowl full of food, and a soft bed. She even got to go for walks around the neighborhood. The "free dog" myth was a reality, but our love for Lucky the Discount Dog was so great that we were happy to see her regain her health and eventually thrive. She was a part of our family for over fifteen years.

As I think about God's grace, I'm reminded of Lucky. She was a mess—lost, wounded, forgotten, and desperate—but we loved her just as she was. Her wounds, physical and mental, were minor when compared to our desire to give her a new life. We immediately treated her wounds; we gave her a home and a reason to live. We loved her as she was, but we refused to leave her that way.

This is a picture of God's sanctifying grace. God loves us just as we are—lost, broken, abused, and hopeless. God, who has been preveniently reaching out to us our whole lives, finally breaks through and redeems us. God takes us just as we are, but God's love doesn't want us to stay as we are. The Spirit of God wants to continue its work in us. God has plans for us— plans for wholeness and healing and plans to provide us a place to join him in his redemptive work in this world. In one way or another, every one of us is Lucky the Discount Dog.

The call to be filled with the Spirit of God rings out from the pages of the New Testament. On the day of Pentecost, as recorded in Acts 2, God forever changed the way people experienced holiness. What was once achieved through the ongoing offering of sacrifices for the sins of the people was now remedied in the death and resurrection of Jesus. Jesus's work through the cross made it possible to deal not only with the effects of sin but also with the source of sin. Through Christ and by the help of the Holy Spirit, God got to the heart of the matter, which is a matter of the heart.

What God begins in our moment of salvation is justification. Relationally we are restored to fellowship with God through the forgiveness of our sins. We are born again (regenerated) and adopted into God's family as dearly beloved sons and daughters. But relational change is not all that God is doing in our salvation. God also begins, in the moment of our salvation, the work of real deep-hearted change. This is not just a matter of taking away the guilt of sin but also the start of disarming sin's power over us. This real change or deep-hearted transformation is the work of the Holy Spirit.

The Spirit of God begins to reveal to us that there is a problem. Sin is more than just the things we say or do in violation of God's law; sin indwells us through a nature that was marred since the fall of humanity (Rom. 7:17). This inherited sin nature is the target of God's sanctifying grace. God loves us and saves us in our sinful and broken condition, but his love is so vast that he does not want to leave us there but to change us, really change us, from the inside out. When Paul writes to the church in Rome he says, "The mind governed by the flesh is death, but the mind governed by the Spirit is life and peace. The mind governed by the flesh is hostile to God; it does not submit to God's law, nor can it do so. Those who are in the realm of the flesh cannot please God" (8:6-8).

When we experience the saving grace of God and are born again, we begin a glorious journey with Christ, being remade into his image. It isn't very long before we discover that though our sins are forgiven, there are still some things in us that need the deeper work of God's grace. God patiently leads us from this moment on to an experience of his sanctifying grace. We inevitably come to a moment in time when we consider the surrender of our whole selves to God and are filled with his Spirit. Again, Paul writes, "For what the law was powerless to do because it was weakened by the flesh, God did by sending his own Son in the likeness of sinful flesh to be a sin offering. And so he condemned sin in the flesh, in order that the righteous requirement of the law might be fully met in us, who do not live according to the flesh but according to the Spirit" (vv. 3-4).

From that moment on, we are invited to walk with Jesus in the power of his Spirit and grow in sanctifying grace. What begins in a moment lasts for a lifetime, until God calls us home.

Lucky the Discount Dog received our love in her broken condition. She finally stopped fighting against our overtures of care and welcomed life in our family. As we learn to know God, we begin to understand that his plan for us will require real change in us. Sometimes the changes are significant, and we want to run away. God finds us, calls us back, and patiently treats our wounds. Eventually, we learn to trust God and to trust in his plans for us. We stop running and learn to sit still as he works with us. We begin to realize that life with God is the best life and that we want to hold nothing back from our loving God.

God's sanctifying grace reminds us that God loves us as we are, even in our sinful condition. In a thousand ways God invites us into a relationship with him. When we choose him, we are not simply God's broken children but through God's sanctifying grace we are made whole and holy. We may look a bit like discount dogs on the outside, but on the inside, we are being made holy as we walk with the Spirit.

The call of Christ to make disciples becomes a reality when the saved and sanctified people of God come together and pursue Jesus's call. We may face setbacks, but although we face challenges to God's call, we can rely on more than human persistence. We can count, once again, on the grace of God— this time God's sustaining grace.

Styrofoam-Cup Gardens and Sustaining Grace

In his book *Way, Truth, Life*, David Busic defines sustaining grace in this way: "That grace which enables us to do what God calls us to do and to live holy lives."[4] He builds this definition from verse 24 of Jude: "To him who is able to keep you from stumbling and to present you before his glorious presence without fault and with great joy . . ."

---

4. David A. Busic, *Way, Truth, Life: Discipleship as a Journey of Grace* (Kansas City: Foundry, 2021), 113.

When I was in elementary school, my second grade teacher taught the basics of plant life, focusing on the importance of water, soil, and sunlight. To reinforce the lesson, the teacher gave each of us a Styrofoam cup, a few seeds, and some potting soil. To the chagrin of the custodial staff, the day came when we directed tiny spoons of dirt into the cups. We then made depressions in the soil with our tiny fingers and dropped the seeds into the hole. The teacher carefully inspected each cup, wrote our names on the outside, and helped us line the cups along the windowsill in the classroom. Each day we would take turns peering into the soil. For a few weeks, it was just a cup of dirt, but one day, the first green shoots began to appear. With careful watering and patience, each of us had a little cup flower to give our mothers for Mother's Day.

It was a grand gesture, blending uncommon elementary patience and the glory of God's creative genius. It was not surprising when one little girl proudly presented her cup flower to her mother announcing, "Mommy, look what me and God did!"

Without question, God's providence created a world where rich soil, adequate light, seeds, and moisture result in growth. Did the little girl play a role? She did indeed. She prepared the soil, planted the seed, set the cup on the windowsill, and watered the plant whenever she was told. She had partnered with God in the miracle of growth. They weren't equal partners, but partners nonetheless.

How instructive this little story becomes as we consider the power of God's sustaining grace. Although the second grade plant project ended with the production of a little flower, God designed the sanctified life to be ever growing. While

God without question plays the greater role, each of us has a role to play as well. About sustaining grace Busic observes that "we must become gardeners."[5] The seeds of holiness are sown in our sanctification, but now we prune and nurture so that these seeds may become full fruit.[6] God has created a salvation plan that includes not only the forgiveness of our sins but also a remedy for our tendency to sin. His sanctifying grace rescues us from the roller-coaster obedience of the newly converted. But to continue growing in the sanctified life requires our involvement. As Busic notes, "Grace means God has done everything we could not do for ourselves, but it does not mean we now become grace consumers who contribute nothing to the relationship. We cooperate with the active grace of God by reordering our lives around those activities, disciplines, and practices that Jesus modeled."[7]

Just as the elementary child learns the rudimentary practices and disciplines of horticulture, the sanctified believer learns the activities and practices of those pursuing Christlikeness. God is making the pursuit of holiness possible, but we are participating as well. Participating with God in our full redemption means that we form new and holy habits that help to sustain us when the pressure is on. This takes time and is always fueled by the Spirit of God.

---

5. Ibid., 122.

6. Ibid., paraphrase of Busic's quotation from N. T. Wright, *After You Believe: Why Christian Character Matters* (New York: HarperCollins, 2010), 196.

7. Ibid., 108.

Sometimes we experience the prevenient grace of God, which brings us to salvation. In time, we seek for and receive God's sanctifying grace. The tendency for many well-intentioned Christians is to see their growth in grace slow at this point, but this was never God's plan. Instead, God invites us to an ongoing pursuit of holiness so that we can join with him in his redeeming work in the world. But what does that ongoing pursuit of holiness look like? That is the focus of this book, but before digging into that, we must first understand more fully God's intention for pouring out all this grace on us. If we want to take on difficult things, if we want to finally live into Jesus's call to be and make disciples, we will invite others to join us. Let's take the next step.

Two
THE POINT OF GRACE
God's Mission and My Purpose

Online shopping has forever changed the way people make purchases. While brick-and-mortar stores are feeling the pain of e-commerce, the construction of brick-and-mortar warehouses is booming. Behemoth structures designed to be staging points for the connection between producer and consumer now dot the landscape. For an online shopper a major frustration is finding that a purchase is stuck in one of these massive warehouses. This sort of warehousing does not do anyone any good. The purchaser does not benefit from the goods purchased, and the seller suffers at the very least a sullied reputation and possibly the loss of revenue.

As we think about the point of God's grace, warehousing proves a helpful analogy. God's grace is not intended to be "warehoused" within us. Rather, God desires that his grace flow into us and then through us to a needy world. God continues to go to extraordinary lengths to bring about our redemption. The grace of God is truly amazing! But the grace of God must not sit on a spiritual shelf within us. Our personal redemption is essential, but it's not the destination of God's grace. In fact, God intends that his grace serve an important purpose *through us* as well as *in us*. What then is the point of all this grace? The point is that we are not merely spectators to the grand story of God's redemption but active participants.

A friend's trip to the Grand Canyon serves as a fitting illustration. My friend had flown over the Grand Canyon many times and witnessed the vast expanse of the American Southwest. Last year, however, when he and his wife traveled by train and visited the canyon in person, his perspective changed dramatically. He experienced firsthand the magnitude of nature along with the sounds, smells, and textures of the national park. In the same way, we must not simply learn about the mission of God but also join other believers in experiencing it firsthand, asking God to show us how to play our part in his glorious mission on earth.

Personal but Not Private

Most people reading this book will acknowledge that we have been taught that the point of the grace of God is our personal relationship with Jesus Christ. While true, this understanding proves incomplete. We should prioritize a personal relationship with Jesus, but we must be careful not to miss the bigger picture. We can, as the old saying goes, miss the forest for the trees. Our focus on a personal relationship reveals that we are products of our era and the influence of evangelical Christianity. This emphasis on a personal relationship with Jesus represents an essential component of God's grace, but the unintended by-product of this emphasis is that our personal salvation becomes *overly* personal.

You might wonder what that means. This can best be summarized in a little phrase that gained popularity in recent years: "Our salvation is personal, just not private." The phrase reminds us that God's amazing grace provides our personal salvation, but God intends more. A facet of our salvation must be *public* or at least shared. Before you feel guilty about another evangelical mainstay—sharing your faith—hear me out. Personal salvation and sharing our faith matter, but they are components of a much larger initiative that resides in the very heart of God. That which resides in the heart of God must be reflected in the life of the God follower. You have a key role in expressing God's heart for this world.

The Mission of God

Cable television can adversely impact movie viewing. With more than a hundred channels to choose from, it is easy to discover a favorite movie after it has already started. Often by the time a person sees a movie in its entirety, he or she has all but forgotten how the story actually began.

We can mistakenly understand the story of God this way. We can have an episodic memory of God's activity in the Scriptures but miss the overarching story. We may, for instance, focus almost entirely on the story of Jesus, and for good reason. The baby of Bethlehem and the cross of Calvary provide the

○ ○ ○

The mission of God is to live in right relationship with creation.

○ ○ ○

fulcrum upon which all of history depends, but the mission of God began long ago. To understand the point of God's grace we must go all the way back to the beginning. Let's go back to the story of creation in Genesis 1 and 2, and in these sacred words discover the answer to the question, What was and is God's mission?

Reading through Genesis 1 and 2, it is not difficult to see that God created out of love and that he desires to live in right relationship with his creation. The imagery of Genesis is rich with the picture of God and creation, especially humanity, living in harmony, united in motive and intention.

Sadly, however, Genesis 3 details the fracturing of this harmony between God and creation. Eve and Adam fall victim to the wiles of the serpent and disobey God's plans for their existence. In the decision to assert their own wills over the will of God, they break the harmony between Creator and creation.

Let's pause a moment and attempt to define the mission of God: the mission of God is to live in right relationship with creation. God desires a relationship of mutual love with us. This mission was broken in the rebellion of humanity, and there was nothing humanity could do to repair it.

At this point, God could have given up, wiped humanity out, and started again or developed another plan. Instead, God desired harmony between Creator and creation and set out to make things whole again. God's mission was and is to live in right relationship with his creation, so God acted next in a very specific way to make that possible again.

Let's take a brief journey through the story of God together. Remember, this is not just an arbitrary history lesson but the foundation upon which our Christian lives are built. What we learn from the past helps us act faithfully in our present and future walk with Jesus. God's mission reveals our mission.

"I Will Make of You a Great Nation"[1]

Genesis 12 reveals God's missional action. Through Abram (whose name was later changed to Abraham), God desired to make a great nation, but not so that Abram could be exalted. Remember, God's mission was and is to live in right relationship with creation. God's purpose in raising up a people of his own was true to his original mission. God would use Abram's descendants as couriers of grace to bear the message of redemption to the world. Through the descendants of Abram, God intended to restore what was broken in Genesis 3, and then creation and all people on earth could be restored to a right relationship with their creator.

The stories of the Old Testament patriarchs—Abraham (Abram), Isaac, and Jacob—all point to this desired end. When God's people were eventually enslaved in Egypt at the hand of a pharaoh who no longer knew Abraham's descendant Joseph, God moved powerfully to free them. God planned to use them to restore his mission of living in right relationship with humanity and ultimately all that he had made.

I love that God chose to work with ordinary people when he raised up Abraham's descendants. People like us played key roles in the mission of God. Here's a little spoiler alert: God is

---

1. Genesis 12:2, ESV.

consistent in the methodology surrounding his mission. When we hold the mission of God in our minds while reading the Old Testament, the stories come alive. In these stories we get the chance to zoom in on the history of God's mission and see his people in all their humanity trying to fulfill the call of God. Rather than seeing the Scriptures as a random collection of ancient Hebrew history, we can slow down and truly feel the weight of God's mission. What's more, as we consider God's actions in history to preserve his mission, we discover that God was passionate about involving people like us in his plans. How exciting to see God's plans unfold before us as we begin to imagine our place in them.

Write These Laws on Your Hearts

The Ten Commandments and the law of God given through Moses make better sense when we see them as God refining his people so that they can fulfill his mission. These laws were not arbitrary rules given to ensure God's people toed the line. Instead, they were standards given to keep God's people in step with God so that the restoration of what was broken in the fall could be pursued through them. Notice again that God has chosen to fulfill his mission through fallible humans like us. When we see God's law in this way, we no longer view God as some sort of cosmic killjoy but instead understand his extraordinary efforts to preserve his original mission.

The law, however, exposes the depths of human depravity. The children of Israel struggled to live up to the law. Looking closely at the story of God's people in the Old Testament, we can feel the tension of Psalm 78, which describes the roll-er-coaster relationship God's own people had with God:

Whenever God slew them, they would seek him;

they eagerly turned to him again.

They remembered that God was their Rock,

that God Most High was their Redeemer.

But then they would flatter him with their mouths,

lying to him with their tongues;

their hearts were not loyal to him,

they were not faithful to his covenant.

Yet he was merciful;

he forgave their iniquities

and did not destroy them.

Time after time he restrained his anger

and did not stir up his full wrath.

He remembered that they were but flesh,

a passing breeze that does not return. (Vv. 34-39)

How comforting for us to see the mercy of God directed toward people who seem much more prone to fumble his mission than they are to fulfill it. As we try to imagine ourselves in the sandals of the Israelites, we need the assurance of our merciful God.

God's mercy is rich, thankfully, and God continued his work to restore what was broken by sin in Genesis 3. Following the conquest of the promised land, God sent prophets who reminded the people of God's ultimate plans. The prophets called the children of Israel back to a right relationship with God. Recalling our discussion earlier in this chapter about personal salvation and its connection to the mission of God, we can see

Israel demonstrating that God's people themselves must first be restored before the mission of God can go forward as God intended.

Let's pause here long enough to look back across the Old Testament and acknowledge the struggle for God's people. The law provided a righteousness that was "outside in." Imagine the prophet Isaiah as a kind of on-the-scene news reporter. Here's his report summarizing the state of God's mission in the hands of Israel: "The Lord says: 'These people come near to me with their mouth and honor me with their lips, but their hearts are far from me. Their worship of me is based on merely human rules they have been taught'" (Isa. 29:13).

The outside-in approach of the law proved inconsistent in fulfilling God's mission despite the best efforts of God's people and his prophets. Thankfully, God's mission did not collapse. God had a new approach. This time God would work from the inside out.

The apostle Paul's words to the church in Rome help us anticipate this transition: "For what the law was powerless to do because it was weakened by the flesh, God did by sending his own Son in the likeness of sinful flesh to be a sin offering. And so he condemned sin in the flesh" (Rom. 8:3).

○ ○ ○

God had not given up on
his mission of redeeming
the world through Israel
but had now offered
himself in the person of
Jesus to accomplish
his purpose.

○ ○ ○

"In These Last Days"[2]

Ultimately, God moved in a singular way to restore his mission on earth. The writer to the Hebrews captures the story like this:

> In the past God spoke to our ancestors through the prophets at many times and in various ways, but in these last days he has spoken to us by his Son, whom he appointed heir of all things, and through whom also he made the universe. The Son is the radiance of God's glory and the exact representation of his being, sustaining all things by his powerful word. After he had provided purification for sins, he sat down at the right hand of the Majesty in heaven. (Heb. 1:1-3)

The apostle John also captures this idea succinctly: "The Word became flesh and made his dwelling among us" (John 1:14).

The incarnation of Jesus, an earthly descendant of David and ultimately of Abraham, embodied God's mission as God's own Son. God had not given up on his mission of redeeming the world through Israel but had now offered himself in the person of Jesus to accomplish his purpose.

Many years ago, we had a beagle named Missy. We kept her tied to her doghouse on our ten-acre farm when we weren't at home to keep her out of mischief. Occasionally we would come home and then leave again quickly. This confused Missy. She would yip and jump and wag her tail, thinking, I suppose, that we would soon unclip her from her rope and spend time

---

2. Hebrews 1:1.

together. Usually, we only had time to offer a wave and a "Missy's a good girl" as we hustled on with our business. I don't know if dogs feel disappointment, but it sure seemed that way. What Missy loved the most, however, was being unclipped from her leash and having us get down on hands and knees to play with her. She practically sang a whimpering joy tune and nearly wagged her tail completely off as she licked our faces and romped with us in the yard.

It was one thing to acknowledge her from a distance but quite another to enter her world, get down on her level, free her from her bonds, and enjoy time together. This helps us understand the next bold move of God to preserve his mission on earth.

Are we destined to fumble God's mission as Israel did? Is there a better hope for us as we not only learn the breadth of God's mission but also find our place in it?

Incarnation and the Mission of God

God's mission is perfectly embodied in the person of Jesus. Jesus is God incarnate, sent to offer redemption at an even deeper level than what the law could provide. What's more, Jesus lived in a right relationship with those he encountered. He modeled the pinnacle of human relationship by embracing obedience in the divine relationship. The "vertical" had an unmistakable impact on the "horizontal." He clearly asserted that his will was to do the will of his Father; the Father's mission determined Jesus's mission (John 4:27-38). Jesus took upon himself Israel's missionary vocation (Matt. 5:17-20), but more than that, Jesus served as the agent of God's salvation to the ends of the earth.

It is beautiful to realize that God's mission of redemption is no longer focused only on the descendants of Abraham. Jesus embodied the mission of God, making it radically visible to all humanity. That means that we have a real hope to be more than just spectators, outsiders looking in on the unfolding plan of God; rather, we are fully accepted as mission bearers for King Jesus.

Frequently, when I'm with my son, people comment on how much we look and act alike. What I usually say in response to these comments is something like, "Yes, I guess we do resemble each other, except he's younger, smarter, more talented, and handsome and has a better sense of humor." From my perspective, it's fun to have a "Mini-Me," but our resemblance pales in comparison to what the Scriptures teach about Jesus and his Father: "The Son is the image of the invisible God, the firstborn over all creation. . . . For God was pleased to have all his fullness dwell in him, and through him to reconcile to himself all things, whether things on earth or things in heaven, by making peace through his blood, shed on the cross" (Col. 1:15, 19-20).

Not only does Jesus show us the Father, but Jesus also embodies the very mission of God! We see in Jesus the ultimate expression God's plans for creation. Jesus is reconciling all things, all the things that Genesis says God created, including all of us, into a right relationship with God.

Crucifixion and the Mission of God

In Jesus's obedience, even to death, the mission of God reached its climax (2 Cor. 5:19). By accomplishing God's purpose for humanity and conquering sin, Jesus not only made salvation freely available to everyone but also made it possible for people to carry out God's redemptive plans. Through Jesus, God and humanity could finally be fully reconciled into a right and life-giving relationship. Jesus's life, teachings, and deeds proclaim the reign of God, and Jesus's death atoned for all that separated people from God. Once and for all, Jesus guaranteed the mission of God. Remember what we learned about grace in chapter 1? Jesus's death and resurrection made that possible.

Why is Jesus's death so essential to God's mission? Because Jesus alone offered the appropriate sacrifice. The death of a self-sacrificing person is certainly beyond commendable from a human perspective, but it fails to "reach" God. The death of God is self-emptying but fails to connect with humanity. It is only in Jesus, fully God and fully human, that the mission of God is recovered. Jesus is God, so his death repairs the brokenness in the relationship between God and humanity and puts God's self-giving love on full display. Jesus is human, so God's righteous redemption reaches all the way to us. In the crucifixion of Jesus, God's mission to live in a right relationship with humanity is not only recovered but also offered to all people. Through Christ, what God intended in Eden is once again possible—the original mission of God to live in harmony with his creation.

Resurrection and the Mission of God

While the cross remains the enduring symbol of Christianity, it is the empty tomb that completes God's redemptive work. In Jesus's resurrection, the grip of sin, death, and the grave is broken. The resurrection means that the power of sin to separate God and humanity is once and for all defeated, and the power of God to enable our obedience is unleashed. What was begun in Eden, the harmony of Creator and created, is once again a reality.

Ascension and the Mission of God

Following his resurrection, Jesus gathered with his disciples, charged them to make disciples, and ascended into heaven before their eyes. In this event the disciples felt both the blessing and the weight of the mission of God. Jesus handed over to his followers the work of proclaiming that a right relationship with God was possible. They struggled to understand this commission and to undertake it, but the assignment had been given.

Just think of it: what began in Eden, was broken in the fall, restarted in Israel, embodied in Jesus, purchased with his death, and sealed in his resurrection was handed over to a group of followers who only hours before had abandoned Jesus in his most desperate hour. The weight of this call undoubtedly paralyzed them as they stood staring into the sky and wondering what to do next.

When we consider our role in God's mission, we can feel overwhelmed. It is a daunting yet essential task for the follower

43

of Jesus. If you are sensing your own Israelite-like weakness, know this: Jesus's death offers the cure for sin's brokenness. His resurrection demonstrates the power of God. The ascension reveals our need for supernatural power, and what God does next makes that power available to all believers.

Pentecost and God's Mission

Gratefully, Jesus's Great Commission was followed by the gift of the Holy Spirit. In Pentecost, God radically changed the way he gave his Spirit. Before Pentecost, God gave his Spirit on occasion in quite specific circumstances or to select leaders. For example, God gave his Spirit to King David. Similarly, Elijah and his successor, Elisha, knew the power of God's Spirit. The judges, too, operated under the power of the Spirit of God.[3] The Holy Spirit was not offered to the rank-and-file follower of God until Pentecost. On this day God decided that all the followers of Jesus would receive the gift of his Spirit. What timing! The mission of God had been handed over to flawed humans. Without the supernatural help of God, the mission of God was doomed to fail. But it did not fail. In fact, the first and greatest revival of God's mission soon followed the gift of the Spirit.

I heard a story of a simple laborer who cut firewood for a living. His friends convinced him to purchase a new chain saw at the local hardware store to improve his life. Not fully understanding his purchase but eager to please his friends and desir-

---

3. See the book of Judges.

ing to cut more firewood with less effort, he gave in and bought the saw. A few days later he returned angrily to the hardware store, slammed the saw on the counter, and demanded his money back. The salesclerk inquired about the problem, and the woodcutter said, "This thing won't cut!" About that time the salesclerk pulled the rope and the saw roared to life! Startled and wide-eyed, the woodcutter said, "What's that noise!"

I love that story because it so clearly demonstrates that without power, the chain saw was ineffective. Without the power of God given in the Holy Spirit on the day of Pentecost, we lack the power to carry out the mission of God given to us as Christ ascended.

God has ensured that we are able to carry out what he has called us to do. His mission is possible because his plans are perfect.

God's Mission and My Purpose

Knowing that God's mission in the world consists of living in harmony with his creation, and knowing the extraordinary lengths to which God has gone to restore this mission, we can come to grips with the reality that God has handed this mission off to us, his followers, and has given us the power of the indwelling Holy Spirit to accomplish the task. It seems clear that our purpose in life, then, is to join together and take up God's mission with all our hearts and, with God's help, to make it a reality.

Ask most people to describe the church and you will hear either a description of the building or a commentary on the worship service. It seems that we have reduced the clear call of Jesus to carry out the mission of God into a weekly routine that we hope will keep us from sin and an eternity without God. But it is clear that God has intentionally made it possible for his mission to be carried out through regular folks like us.

We live between Pentecost and the return of Christ. Rather than simply gazing into the eastern sky awaiting Jesus's return, there is something important for us to do. Our primary task as God's people is to live in harmony with God and others. God's mission is about salvation—ours and that of everyone we meet. It is a plan for reconciliation with God made possible by the death and resurrection of Jesus. God graciously invites us to participate with him in the restoration work of his age-old mission.

Our churches are populated with redeemed people, but we cannot miss the reality that we are sent out into the world to proclaim Christ. The mission of God for the church is to spread this good news. Jesus points to discipleship and calls us to join him in his mission of redemption.

I'm a fan of Harley-Davidson motorcycles. I own one myself and ride it whenever I can. I recently learned in a podcast by the curator of the Harley-Davidson Museum that from the very beginning of the company, its leaders set aside one example of each model for posterity. Many of these motorcycles have never been ridden for more than a few feet as they were moved into storage. While all Harley fans applaud the foresight of the company founders to preserve one of the iconic brands of our era, there is something about a motorcycle that isn't ridden that bothers me. No one has had the joy of throwing a leg over that machine and rumbling off into adventure. No one has experienced the sights, sounds, and smells that are unique to riding that bike. It seems that the very purpose for the machine's existence is somehow lost in its nonuse. A motorcycle's primary function is, after all, transportation and not just art.

Our primary function is to follow Jesus. God had a plan in creation and made the recovery of that plan possible through Jesus. That plan has been handed over to those of us who have met Jesus and had our lives transformed by his grace. Now is not the time to permit our redeemed lives to be stowed away for posterity. Now is the time to take up the commission of Jesus and give ourselves wholeheartedly to the mission of God. God's plan depends on us. With the help of the Spirit of God, we must carry the redemptive message of Jesus to those around us. A Christian's primary function is, after all, mission and not just eternity.

What kinds of people take up this charge? The Bible has a name for them, disciples. Disciples are people of grace, and discipleship is what we call the adventure of following Jesus.

three
THE PEOPLE OF GRACE
What Is a Disciple?

Have you ever noticed that despite the many different breeds of dogs in the world, we can identify a dog as a dog even when we don't know its breed? Chihuahuas and English mastiffs are vastly different in size and appearance, but we can tell that both are dogs because they share the same basic identifiable traits. Christians come in all shapes and sizes too. Some are quiet and reserved; some, louder and more boisterous. Some dress formally, and others casually. Some like pianos and organs, and some prefer guitars and drums. Christians are very different, but we, like our four-legged friends, share some basic and identifiable traits too. Christians are followers of Jesus, and followers of Jesus embrace God's grace, striving to become like him. This quest defines our existence. Followers of Jesus also sense an urgency to help others along in their journey of grace.

If you've ever gone hiking and camping with friends, you can identify with the inevitable "gathering of stuff" meeting that usually takes place. You have a tent; your friend has an extra sleeping pad. Someone else brings the camp stove and cooking utensils. You don't really need duplicate gear, but you want to be sure you have just what you need for the journey ahead. Perhaps it would help us to pause a minute and examine our supplies.

In chapter 1, we discussed the reach of God's amazing grace and then, in chapter 2, the importance of God's all-encompassing mission. Before going any farther on our journey together, let's "gather our stuff" and be sure we are ready for the rest of our journey, particularly as it impacts the question of this chapter: What is a disciple?

The Vertical and Horizontal of Discipleship

As a preteen, my parents let me move my bedroom into our unfinished basement. I found an old carpet remnant, put my box spring and mattress on the floor, set up my stereo system, and moved in. I even found an old tube-style TV that worked but needed the occasional adjustment. Nearly every time I turned it on after it had been off for several hours, the picture would roll either vertically or horizontally until I located the adjustment knobs for vertical hold and horizontal hold and dialed them in just right. What an expression of preteen independence to then enjoy the two channels that the ancient rabbit-ear antenna could pick up in my underground (young) man cave!

Like an old television from the 1970s, discipleship has both an important vertical element and an important horizontal element. Being a disciple according to Scripture clearly means that a person is a follower of Jesus. When Jesus called Andrew, Simon Peter, James, and John, the Bible says they left their nets and followed him. When we hear the call of Jesus to forsake our sins and receive his forgiveness, we hear his call to follow. If you pick up the analogy from my old TV, following Jesus is the "vertical" adjustment we make in our lives. We choose to unite with our Father who is in heaven (the vertical relationship) by the sacrifice of his Son, Jesus, and with the help of the Holy Spirit. But discipleship also has a horizontal element. As we noted in the section on the mission of God, Jesus handed his ministry over to his disciples as he ascended. Jesus invited them, and ultimately all his followers, to carry on his work "horizontally." This means we take up Jesus's mission and begin to invite others to join us in the journey of grace.

Being a disciple gives full expression to the Great Commandment that anchored Jesus's response to the Pharisees in Matthew 22:37-39: "'Love the Lord your God with all your heart and with all your soul and with all your mind.' This is the first and greatest commandment. And the second is like it: 'Love your neighbor as yourself.'" We can so easily see the vertical and horizontal components of the call to discipleship.

Consider this summary that sets us up for the journey ahead: A disciple responds to God's *prevenient grace* by accepting the offer of *saving grace*. A disciple becomes aware of and then accepts God's offer of *sanctifying grace* and grows in Christlikeness because of God's *sustaining grace*. Then a disciple

○ ○ ○

We call the process
of growing in our
relationship with God
and inviting others along
with us in the journey of
grace *discipleship.*

○ ○ ○

takes up the mission of God to join with God in helping someone else along his or her journey of grace. A disciple is a person of grace. We call the process of growing in our relationship with God and inviting others along with us in the journey of grace *discipleship.*

This is a helpful and realistic definition of discipleship. It keeps the focus on God's grace and yet invites our participation. Unfortunately, many of us get discouraged as we measure our lives against the clear call of Jesus. Although we remember Jesus's call to make disciples, many of us feel ineffective at carrying it out. We know what is expected of us, but we haven't been very good at it, so we simply ignore the problem. Maybe part of our struggle is that we have undertaken it largely on our own. More on that later, but for now, let's examine this problem together.

A Problem in the Pews

The church I pastor resembles many churches. The congregation offers a wide variety of programming and raises enough money to have a balanced budget and share in the global ministry of the denomination. We have the usual ministries for a church our size and pastors to oversee them. When people attend, they receive a warm greeting, and most leave having had a good experience. By the standards of our tribe, our church does well.

Although our church has many positive traits, it is troubling that we see fewer new converts than we wish and that the number of people passionate about following Christ seems about the same year after year. In many cases, members of our church can recite the books of the Bible and may even be fluent in Bible stories, but some fail to connect the dots between the lessons of Sunday school and the scriptural implications for life in a complex world. For instance, what do the stories of the Bible teach us about the grace of our loving God? As we witness God's mission unfolding in the pages of the text, how can we apply this biblical message to our lives?

Although Christians in our church regularly employ historical and critical thinking in their non-church lives, they struggle to employ this kind of in-depth analysis in their lives of faith.[1] Consequently, what they know historically, and perhaps even what they believe, fails to reframe their lives against the backdrop of mainstream culture. Churches often suffer from what J. I. Packer and Gary A. Parrett describe as "a case of being so close yet so far away . . . like a shower of arrows that all hit the target yet miss the bull's-eye."[2] As a result, many churches suffer from a form of discipleship that could be described as *a mile wide and an inch deep.*

Without question, the cultural forces surrounding the church produce an impact on the church. Hundreds of ideologies beset us daily, all vying for our allegiance. If we decide to stop for a moment and assess our lives, we can see the impact of this onslaught. The church seems beset with what eighteenth-century pastor John Wesley called "dissipation," or being so busy with

---

1. James Carroll, *Jerusalem, Jerusalem: How the Ancient City Ignited Our Modern World* (New York: Houghton Mifflin, 2011), 189-90; quoted in Jack L. Seymour, *Teaching the Way of Jesus: Educating Christians for Faithful Living* (Nashville: Abingdon Press, 2014), 43.

2. J. I. Packer and Gary A. Parrett, *Grounded in the Gospel: Building Believers the Old-Fashioned Way* (Grand Rapids: Baker Books, 2010), 9.

life's concerns that congregants have little capacity for attention to the things of the spiritual life.[3] This neglect of growth in the direction of transformation presents a larger concern when we realize this unique challenge in nearly all evangelical expressions of the church.[4] For all of our efforts in ministry, we must ask ourselves, are we really making disciples who are passionately following Jesus and inviting others along on the journey of grace? Have we misunderstood that the purpose of the church is to help people become people of grace or disciples? Our congregations should be growing to the point that they are helping others along in their journey of grace, but instead they tend to leave spiritual growth up to church attendance and chance, and the call to make disciples goes unheeded.

This book proposes a way to capture our congregations' imaginations and invite them into a refreshed expression of the vibrant life of following Christ. We will explore this further as we proceed, but for now let's pause and examine the problem.

The Participation Problem

While well documented in the last decade by several research groups,[5] a conversation with most pastors or church

---

3. Henry H. Knight III, *The Presence of God in the Christian Life: John Wesley and the Means of Grace* (Lanham, MD: The Scarecrow Press, 1987), 32. Here Knight is quoting from Wesley's *An Earnest Appeal to Men of Reason and Religion.*

4. George Barna, *America at the Crossroads: Explosive Trends Shaping America's Future and What You Can Do about It* (Grand Rapids: Baker Books, 2016), 31-37.

5. These research groups include the Barna Group, the American Culture and Faith Institute, the Pew Research Center, and the American Religious Identification Survey.

leaders will eventually result in a similar sentiment: the American church is struggling. The cited causes for the struggle may vary, but one thing everyone can agree on is that over the past fifty years, the levels of participation have trended downward. The American Culture and Faith Institute (ACFI) reveals that in 2016 barely one out of ten adults attended a Sunday school class or a small group. This decline in what has traditionally functioned as the discipleship arm of American churches resembles the decline in worship-service attendance over the same period. Join this with a general decline in Bible reading and one can see why George Barna quips, "These certainly aren't the good old days of religious instruction by any stretch of the imagination."[6]

Consider these statistics: In the last twenty years, church attendance has declined by 21 percent. During that same period, small group participation has dropped by 28 percent and Sunday school participation has declined by 29 percent.[7] The Pew Research Center recently reported that based on its research, the number of people reporting no religious affiliation, the so-called nones, more than doubled between the years of 1990 and 2012, from 15 percent to 34 percent. This has led James Emery White to conclude that "America is not a Christian nation. This does not mean it is non-Christian or anti-Christian, simply that it has joined the ranks of many other

6. Barna, *America at the Crossroads*, 44-47.
7. Ibid., 47.

Western countries and is *post*-Christian."[8] The church, without question, has a participation problem.

To summarize, churches are struggling to engage people in the primary discipleship venues of Sunday school and small groups. The clarion call of Jesus seems diminished to a kind of melancholy background music. How wonderful if we could find a way to once again trumpet Jesus's call to be and make disciples! God's grace is not diminished, and God's mission has not changed, but our ability to carry out God's plans effectively is suffering.

While participation numbers may not be a completely reliable indicator of the overall discipleship in our churches, if declining participation in the historic discipleship settings of the church teaches us anything, we need a discipleship renewal. When the church fails to produce passionate followers of Jesus (disciples) and fails to engage with others who are on the journey of grace (discipleship), we have mishandled the mission of God. The progress of God's mission to live in a right relationship with the ever-increasing number of people on earth not only stalls but also loses ground. As discipleship author Bill Hull often quips, "Churches exist for the primary purpose of making disciples, and those disciples are meant to be a gift to the world."[9] We are the church, and we simply cannot fail to recover the mission of God and move it forward by the grace of God.

---

8. James Emery White, *The Rise of the Nones: Understanding and Reaching the Religiously Unaffiliated* (Grand Rapids: Baker Books, 2014), 43-45.

9. Bill Hull, *Conversion and Discipleship: You Can't Have One without the Other* (Grand Rapids: Zondervan, 2016), 174.

The Pastoral Problem

One of the most alarming components of lackluster discipleship is captured in George Barna's insistence that church leaders seem satisfied with their level of discipleship emphasis. "Surveys among pastors reveal them to be quite pleased with the spiritual condition of their congregants and planning to continue on the same course of action to keep producing the same outcomes they have been generating."[10] Like the archer who fires an arrow and then quickly runs to it and paints a target around it, perhaps pastors have learned to lower expectations to match outcomes rather than to come face-to-face with the extent of the problem.

It appears that pastors and church leaders have been bitten by the bug of consumerism. Instead of finding ways to measure discipleship in the local church in order to gauge its health and find ways to improve, church leaders seem content to measure attendance, donations, program involvement, staff expansion, and space requirements. The assumption is that an increase in bodies, programs, dollars, employees, and square footage reflects a dynamic, healthy, growing ministry through which lives are being changed. Unfortunately, research within and across churches demonstrates that these assumptions are faulty: virtually no correlation exists between those factors and life transformation.[11]

---

10. Barna, *America at the Crossroads*, 63.
11. Ibid., 64.

Barna relates that an enormous research project designed to trace "the spiritual development of Americans who identify as Christians revealed that genuine spiritual transformation is shockingly rare."[12] The church doesn't appear to lack the necessary resources for life transformation, but it does appear to need a priority adjustment. Disciples are not likely to be formed in the consumer mindset of bigger, better, and more.

At stake is not merely the fate of the organized church but more importantly God's redemptive mission in the world. When Jesus quoted Isaiah 61:1-2 in reference to himself in the synagogue at Nazareth, he was invoking the dramatic reversal of the forces of darkness that had been proclaimed by the Old Testament prophets:

The Spirit of the Lord is on me,

because he has anointed me

to proclaim good news to the poor.

He has sent me to proclaim freedom for the prisoners

and recovery of sight for the blind,

to set the oppressed free,

to proclaim the year of the Lord's favor. (Luke 4:18-19)

The significance of this moment is that Jesus declared he would not only lead this renewal but also embody it. Jesus was announcing the inbreaking of a new kingdom, one built not on power and wealth but on sacrifice and love. Jesus was embodying the grand mission of God and began to teach his disciples to seek the fulfillment of this mission even as they prayed,

---

12. Ibid.

59

saying, "Our Father in heaven, hallowed be your name, your kingdom come, your will be done, on earth as it is in heaven" (Matt. 6:9-10).

Jesus's life and teachings clearly point to this kingdom's arrival and advancement, but Christians today look around to acknowledge that what was begun over two thousand years ago is yet to be completed. Indeed, the preceding discussion of the church's struggles to take up God's mission even when empowered by his grace can be disheartening.

Have you ever watched one of those movies where the pilot of an airplane unexpectedly becomes incapacitated and one of the passengers must pilot the plane? The passenger is strapped into the cockpit and fumbles for the headset as sweat beads form on his or her brow. The nearest airport tower locates an experienced flier to relay moment-by-moment instructions to the frantic passenger-pilot, who, in true Hollywood fashion, miraculously lands the plane and saves the day. If you've ever imagined yourself in that situation while watching a film, you might be ready for the reality of God's plan.

The biblical narrative declares that God has chosen to entrust the future of his kingdom into the hands of ordinary believers. What an overwhelming reality! The Scriptures and the Holy Spirit offer us moment-by-moment instructions, and yet many Christians today are so steeped in the busyness of life and even church activity that the realities of this mission escape their attention. No one seems to be piloting the cause of discipleship, and the results are obvious. Further, even those who are aware of God's unfolding work struggle to imagine themselves adequate to the task of being a copilot with God.

○ ○ ○

Without disciples, the
church loses sight of the
reason for which Jesus
came and thus deprives
the world of the
good news.

○ ○ ○

David Lowes Watson has authored numerous books and articles linking the call of Christ to make disciples with the work of John Wesley. He writes,

> If Christians are to understand their role, therefore, and undertake their task with integrity, they must not evade the mysteries of God's salvation; nor must they try to resolve them. Christians must rather seek to join with the risen Christ *in the midst* of the mysteries, proclaiming the hope of the gospel. They must work faithfully in the world, waiting expectantly for God's redemption to be fulfilled, and wrestling with the tensions of a message which points to the future. To do all of this, they must be centered on Christ, empowered by the Holy Spirit; and they must be formed into faithful, obedient disciples. Nothing less will suffice.[13]

Disciples, therefore, are the hope of the church. Without disciples, the church loses sight of the reason for which Jesus came and thus deprives the world of the *good news*. Such a cause is too important to be mishandled and thereby stalled.

Jesus very clearly called disciples and handed that call over to the church in Matthew 28:19-20: "Therefore go and make disciples of all nations, baptizing them in the name of the Father and of the Son and of the Holy Spirit, and teaching

---

13. David Lowes Watson, *Forming Christian Disciples: The Role of Covenant Discipleship and Class Leaders in the Congregation* (Nashville: Discipleship Resources, 1991), 5. See also by David Lowes Watson: *Covenant Discipleship: Christian Formation through Mutual Accountability* (Eugene, OR: Wipf and Stock, 1998), *Accountable Discipleship: Handbook for Covenant Discipleship Groups in the Congregation* (Nashville: Discipleship Resources, 1984), and *Class Leaders: Recovering a Tradition* (Eugene, OR: Wipf and Stock, 1998).

them to obey everything I have commanded you. And surely I am with you always, to the very end of the age."

We have noted the mixed track record of faithfulness to both this call and commission. David Lowes Watson continues: "Yet there have always been those who have responded to the Jewish carpenter with integrity. Not only have their spiritual gifts been much in evidence, but their faithfulness and obedience to the teachings of Jesus have provided us with important role models for Christian discipleship. . . . The early Methodist revival was such a time."[14]

John Wesley's Methodists understood, after their founder, that as Christians, the purposes of God in the world had been handed over to them and that to prove faithful they would need a serious-minded pursuit of God. This focused approach repeatedly drove Wesley back to the Scriptures as the primary witness to God's intentions. Wesley frequently spoke of God's work in redemption as a recovery of God's original intentions for humanity. In the essay *A Further Appeal to Men of Reason and Religion*, Wesley sought "a restoration of the soul to its primitive health . . . the renewal of our souls after the image of God, in righteousness and true holiness, in justice, mercy, and truth."[15]

You might be wondering what an eighteenth-century pastor in England could possibly teach twenty-first-century Chris-

---

14. Watson, *Forming Christian Disciples*, 7.

15. John Wesley, *A Further Appeal to Men of Reason and Religion*, in *The Works of John Wesley*, ed. Thomas Jackson, 3rd ed. (London: Wesleyan Methodist Book Room, 1872; repr., Peabody, MA: Hendrickson, 1984), 8:47.

tians. In the pages ahead I'll offer a brief rationale for Wesley as a reliable voice, but for now consider a quick illustration.

Have you ever piloted a rowboat? I don't mean a kayak or canoe; I mean a rowboat complete with oars mounted on both the starboard (right) and port (left) rails of the boat. If you've ever taken up those oars and rowed the boat, you will remember that although the boat's front, or bow, is often tapered to permit it to slice through the water easily, the oars work best when the one piloting the boat faces backward, toward the stern. Indeed, facing the stern and pulling on the oars brings about the most power and efficiency in rowing. Can you picture it? As you row the boat forward, you're facing rearward. Let's consider John Wesley and his work with new converts in England so long ago in that light. The pages ahead will move us forward in our quest for effective discipleship, but let's keep an eye on Wesley and his example. So effective was his ministry that the early Methodists not only changed the church but also impacted an entire nation.

four
CHALLENGES
TO GRACE
Why Is Discipleship So Difficult?

We've probably all watched videos of salmon swimming upstream. Maybe some of you have even witnessed this firsthand. We marvel at the instinct to return to the waters from which they were hatched to lay their eggs, thus giving the tiny fingerlings the best chance of survival. If you've ever tried to imitate swimming upstream in a river or even fallen victim to the imperceptible drift that occurs while swimming in the ocean, you know that the journey against the current is daunting. It is no small miracle that the salmon complete the annual journey and that the species continues.

The cause of discipleship—our growing in Christlikeness and inviting others along on the journey of grace—feels so challenging, kind of like swimming against the current. The forces of our culture flow away from God and his purposes for the most part. We must not forget that Jesus spoke of this when he said, "I have told you these things, so that in me you may have peace. In this world you will have trouble. But take heart! I have overcome the world" (John 16:33).

Notice that while acknowledging the struggle, Jesus also offers us a reminder of his power. Thank God for his grace that enables us not only to survive the cultural currents but also to swim against them and carry on the work Jesus gave us to do. Let's remember Jesus's words even as we try to understand why discipleship can feel so difficult.

The videocassette recorder (VCR) revolutionized home entertainment in the 1980s. Our households suddenly had the ability not only to record television shows and movies from our TVs but also to show movies once reserved for the theater. I was a high school student when the church my father pastored gave him a VCR for Christmas. I'll never forget the oohs and aahs that accompanied the unwrapping in front of the church. It was a glorious machine, complete with a remote control and a digital clock. The clock housed in the VCR was essential because you could program the machine to record your favorite program even when you weren't at home. What electronic wizardry! However, the clock proved very difficult to set, and anytime there was a power outage the clock would reset and blink "12:00 p.m." Soon we discovered that we weren't alone in the struggle to keep the clock set properly. In nearly every home we visited, it was always 12:00 p.m., according to the homeowner's VCR. That crazy clock was not only complicated to set but also demanded a lot of effort to keep set.

Being a disciple and inviting someone else along on the discipleship journey against the currents of culture is kind of like that. It's complicated because of the diverse ideologies surrounding us, and it demands a lot of effort to keep going against that backdrop. As a result, many well-intentioned Christians get discouraged and give up. If there was a visible digital readout on our souls, the display might perpetually blink "Too Difficult." Perhaps understanding what we are up against will help us strategize a way forward.

A Postmodern Secular Worldview

Recent research[1] has determined that America is largely post-Christian and has moved into a postmodern and secular worldview. What is most surprising about this reality is the rapid pace at which it has occurred. In 2005, two-thirds of American adults said that their religious faith was very important to them. Just *ten years* later that had slipped to only half.[2] In just a decade, the cultural currents changed the religious landscape around us.

James White quotes a Barna Group survey in which respondents were asked to indicate their reaction to fifteen measurements of their faith and participation in religious activities. "To be deemed 'post-Christian,' the person had to meet 60 percent or more of the fifteen factors. To be deemed 'highly post-Christian,' the person had to meet at least 80 percent

---

1. This consists of research from the American Culture Faith Institute and the results of the American Religious Identification Survey.

2. Barna, *America at the Crossroads*, 25. See also White, *Rise of the Nones*, 44.

O O O

Discipleship renewal is
essential if the church
hopes to carry out its
God-given mission.

O O O

(twelve or more) of the factors. Examining these fifteen measures of nonreligiosity, they found that 37 percent of Americans are generally post-Christian, and one in four (25 percent) are highly post-Christian."[3]

It is tempting to write these findings off as pertaining largely to those outside the church; indeed, the study was done to try and discover the origins of the "nones." However, Barna points out that although born-again Americans may participate at a higher rate in religious activities, when measuring lifestyle behaviors "the research consistently reveals little discernible difference in the core behaviors and lifestyle attitudes and values of born-again Christians when compared to other Americans."[4]

All of this seems to indicate that the cultural trends in America today are pervasive not only for the average American but also for those who identify as Christian and evangelical. Has the lack of emphasis on discipleship caused this slide in religious identification? Or is the lack of emphasis on discipleship a symptom of the religious landscape? It's the classic "chicken and egg" question, isn't it? We can make the case that the struggling discipleship in our churches is both a symptom and a cause of the negative statistics in religious identification. Regardless of our perspective on that, however, discipleship renewal is essential if the church hopes to carry out its God-given mission. We may be living in a so-called post-Christian land, but we must never forget that Jesus and twelve friends changed

---

3. White, *Rise of the Nones*, 44.
4. Barna, *America at the Crossroads*, 63.

the world through the practice of grace-filled, mission-focused discipleship.

These statistics are not only alarming to church leaders but also sickening, according to Andrew Root. Referencing Charles Taylor's lectures titled "The Malaise of Modernity," Root describes a "low-grade cultural stomachache" of pastors and church leaders today. While his analogy is a bit tongue-in-cheek, pastors report the sentiment of a "nagging illness, the source of which can't be identified."[5] Pastors are firsthand witnesses to the decline of church participation and have the battle scars to prove they have engaged the culture wars, but their training for ministry seems tooled for a time long forgotten.[6] At least for our pastors, the malaise around how to minister in a post-Christian world is tangible.

Before you throw up your hands in frustration and walk away, remember the rowboat. Remember to keep straining forward while looking back first to Jesus and then to John Wesley. This posture marks the way forward for us. Let's not forget that God's grace makes it possible for us to be disciples, and disciples pursue God even as they invite others along on the journey of grace. This journey of grace is the best expression of the mission of God for Christians today.

History teaches us that there have always been threats to the church. Sometimes a threat takes the form of an empire. Other times threats look like ideologies. The mission of God al-

---

5. Andrew Root, *The Pastor in a Secular Age: Ministry to People Who No Longer Need a God* (Grand Rapids: Baker Academic, 2019), 5.

6. Ibid.

ways seems to be a generation away from extinction. Although the gospel of Jesus really is *good news*, it would be shortsighted to ignore the bad news around us. An amusing meme illustrates this well. It depicts a man happily tapping away at a computer, oblivious to the fact that the office in which he is working is on fire. There are threats to the church today, but remember the words of Jesus: "But take heart! I have overcome the world" (John 16:33).

Secularization, Privatization, and Pluralization

According to James White, sociologist Peter Berger has for many years insisted that the church is "being shaped by three deep and fast-moving cultural currents: secularization, privatization, and pluralization."[7] *Secularization* means that "the church is losing its influence as a shaper of life and thought in the wider social order, and Christianity is losing its place as the dominant worldview."[8] *Privatization* means that "a chasm is created between the public and private spheres of life, and spiritual things are increasingly placed within the private arena."[9] *Pluralization* says that "individuals are confronted with a staggering number of ideologies and faith options competing for their attention."[10] These insights are illuminating. No wonder being and making disciples seems so challenging.

---

7. White, *Rise of the Nones*, 45.
8. Ibid., 46.
9. Ibid., 48.
10. Ibid., 49.

If James White and Peter Berger are correct, and the statistics from Barna and others seem to indicate that they are, then the powerful trends of post-Christian America have created a vacuum in the hearts and minds of people where faith and religious participation used to hold sway. Americans, and American evangelicals, are increasingly secularized, privatized, and pluralized. "The declining social significance of religion will inevitably cause a decline in the *number* of religious people and the *extent* to which those people are religious. When society no longer supports religious affirmation, the difficulty of maintaining individual faith increases dramatically."[11] It has been said that nature abhors a vacuum; so does ideology.

Each autumn, we spend a Saturday cleaning up the landscaping around our house. The bright greens and supple blossoms of spring and summer get replaced by the brittle texture and brown colors of fall. We rake and trim, pulling out the dead foliage that only a few weeks before beautified our property. Winter comes and everything is dormant, at least where we live. When spring eventually begins to emerge, everything comes to life—including weeds. The wise gardener knows that the same flower bed that lay dormant all winter will soon be overrun with weeds unless something else gets planted there. Even then, the battle with the unwelcome weeds rages on week after week. Consider how the weeds in your garden are like a particularly potent alternative system of belief that imperceptibly grows in the culture around us.

---

11. Ibid., 47.

The Pull of Consumerism

In the space created by post-Christendom, an alternative "religion" has emerged, the religion of consumerism. "Consumerism is the idea that increasing the consumption of goods and services purchased in the market is always a desirable goal and that a person's well-being and happiness depend fundamentally on obtaining consumer goods and material possessions."[12] John de Graaf, David Wann, and Thomas H. Naylor, in their best-selling book *Affluenza: How Overconsumption Is Killing Us—and How We Can Fight Back,* view consumerism almost like a pathology: "A powerful virus has infected American society, threatening our wallets, our friendships, our families, our communities, and our environment. We call the virus *affluenza.*"[13] The authors continue:

> In our view, the affluenza epidemic is rooted in the obsessive, *almost religious* quest for economic expansion that has become the core principle of what is called the American dream. It's rooted in the fact that our supreme measure of national progress is that quarterly ring of the cash register we call the gross domestic product. It's rooted in the idea that every generation will be materially wealthier than its predecessor and that, somehow, each of us can pursue

---

12. Investopedia, s.v. "Consumerism," by Adam Hayes, last modified July 31, 2022, https://www.investopedia.com/terms/c/consumerism.asp.

13. John de Graaf, David Wann, and Thomas H. Naylor, *Affluenza: How Overconsumption Is Killing Us—and How We Can Fight Back,* 3rd ed. (San Francisco: Berrett-Koehler, 2014), 1.

that single-minded end without damaging the countless other things we hold dear.[14]

If one questions the qualification of consumerism as religion, look again at consumerism's definition. Consumerism says "that a person's *well-being and happiness* depend" on the consumption of goods and services—a message clearly at odds with the Scriptures. Note just these few examples:

- "May the God of hope fill you with all joy and peace as you trust in him, so that you may overflow with hope by the power of the Holy Spirit" (Rom. 15:13).
- "Take delight in the LORD, and he will give you the desires of your heart" (Ps. 37:4).
- "I have told you this so that my joy may be in you and that your joy may be complete" (John 15:11).

De Graaf and company agree, describing the shopping center as the American place of worship: "The Mall of America is more than metaphorically a cathedral; some people get married there. It is also a world-class affluenza hot zone."[15] Note this disturbing detail: "In the Age of Affluenza (as we believe the century following World War II will eventually be called), shopping centers have supplanted churches as a symbol of cultural values. In fact, 70 percent of us visit malls each week, more than attend houses of worship."[16]

---

14. Ibid., 2; emphasis added.

15. Ibid., 17.

16. New Road Map Foundation in partnership with Norwest Environment Watch, *All Consuming Passion: Waking Up from the American Dream* (Seattle: New Road Map Foundation, 1998), 6; cited in De Graaf, Wann, and Naylor, *Affluenza*, 15.

○ ○ ○

Consumerism is the religion of post-Christian America, and it is deeply seated.

○ ○ ○

Jesus came to offer life abundant to be sure, but Americans appear to prefer the alternative religion of consumerism as their means to the abundant life.

Victor Lebow, in 1955, wrote what has become the touchstone for the consumerist mindset and the apparent template for the economic ideals of America. Consider his "religious" language, and bear in mind that this philosophy has had decades to permeate the American culture, aided by the powers of marketing and technology:

> Our enormously productive economy demands that we make consumption *our way of life*, that we convert the buying and use of goods into *rituals, that we seek our spiritual satisfactions*, our ego satisfactions, in consumption. The measure of social status, of social acceptance, of prestige, is now to be found in our consumptive patterns. *The very meaning and significance of our lives today is expressed in consumptive terms.* The greater the pressures upon the individual to conform to safe and accepted social standards, the more does he tend to express his aspirations and his individuality in terms of what he wears, drives, eats—his home, his car, his pattern of food serving, his hobbies.[17]

Consumerism is the religion of post-Christian America, and it is deeply seated. According to sociologist Steve Bruce, "To be sustained and kept intact, [a religion] must be cultivated and guarded. When it is very widely shared and thoroughly

---

17. Victor Lebow, "Price Competition in 1955," reprinted at *Not Buying Anything* (blog), accessed August 22, 2020, https://notbuyinganything.blogspot.com/p/price-competition-in-1955-victor-lebow_27.html; emphasis added.

embedded in everyday life and in powerful social institutions, there is little danger it will disappear."[18] Clearly, this consumer culture is for all practical purposes here to stay.

The challenge is clear. The practice of consumers in a consumeristic culture constitutes an alternative religion with extensive impact. James K. A. Smith retells this story from the Kenyon College commencement address of David Foster Wallace: "There are these two young fish swimming along and they happen to meet an older fish swimming the other way, who nods at them and says 'Morning, boys. How's the water?' And the two young fish swim on for a bit, and then eventually one of them looks over at the other and goes 'What the [heck] is water?'"[19] Smith admonishes people to become aware of their immersions. Consumerism ingrained in a consumer culture is literally the water that Americans swim in.

Our Hometowns

I live in the suburbs in the Kansas City metro area. My neighborhood is like most suburbs in the United States. People drive nice cars, live in safe homes or apartments, and are reasonably educated.

Our cities contain metro parks, and the boutique coffee shops are filled with people using smartphones, laptops, and tablets and sipping six-dollar caffeine beverages. While the

---

18. Steve Bruce, *God Is Dead: Secularization in the West* (Oxford, UK: Blackwell, 2002), 147; quoted in White, *Rise of the Nones*, 48.

19. James K. A. Smith, *You Are What You Love: The Spiritual Power of Habit* (Grand Rapids: Brazos Press, 2016), 38.

culture seems pleasant and passive, it possesses great power. Like most of America, this culture champions wealth, power, and status. Pressure to conform to cultural norms is subtle but strong, and outsiders seem to stand out immediately. While it may wear the garb of the middle class, this culture's tendency toward self-sufficiency traces its origin back to the garden of Eden. Our church is situated right in the center of this culture like a boulder amid a roaring river.

Affluenza offers the following summary of America that fits our hometown like a glove, but regardless of your specific locale, chances are you are no stranger to the authors' conclusions:

> America's 114 million households . . . contain and consume more stuff than all other households throughout history, put together. Behind closed doors, we churn through manufactured goods and piped-in entertainment as if life were a stuff-eating contest. Despite tangible indications of indigestion, we keep consuming, partly because we're convinced it's normal. Writes the columnist Ellen Goodman, "Normal is getting dressed in clothes that you buy for work, driving through traffic in a car that you are still paying for, in order to get to the job that you need so you can pay for the clothes, car and the house that you leave empty all day in order to afford to live in it."[20]

All of this to say that while there are no placards reading "First Church of Consumption" or "Consumerism Assembly," the grip of consumerism on the souls of our neighbors remains strong.

---

20. De Graaf, Wann, and Naylor, *Affluenza*, 33; Ellen Goodman, as quoted in New Road Map Foundation, *All Consuming Passion*, chap. 1, n. 3.

The implications of consumerism are important to the cause of discipleship. Churchgoers suffer from what T. Scott Daniels calls, "'we' confusion."[21] Daniels contends that church folk identify more with their immediate culture than with the culture of Christ's kingdom. George Barna summarizes the situation when he writes:

> When all the smoke and mirrors are removed from the discussion, most churchgoing people in America have no idea what the objectives of their religious pursuits are other than to be a better person, to believe in the existence and goodness of Jesus Christ, to keep God happy, and to be a good church member. When pushed to describe in practical terms what these things mean and how they can best accomplish these objectives, alarmingly few people possess viable answers and almost nobody has a plan. They assume that attending church regularly, praying and reading the Bible occasionally, and completing a church program or two designed to facilitate "spiritual maturity" will do the job.[22]

It appears that the history and implications of the gospel have fallen victim to the ever-present pull of consumerism, and the gospel has been undercut in its transformational influence.

---

21. T. Scott Daniels, *Embracing Exile: Living Faithfully as God's Unique People in the World* (Kansas City: Beacon Hill Press, 2017), 98-102.

22. Barna, *America at the Crossroads*, 64.

Rival Kingdoms

The Kansas City Chiefs is the hometown team where I live. The team is one of the oldest in football and has a proud tradition. In today's competitive marketing environment, most teams develop a slogan or an alternate name annually to pump up sales of T-shirts and bumper stickers. The Cleveland Browns has its "Dawg Pound," the Pittsburgh Steelers of yesteryear had its "Steel Curtain" defense. A few years ago, the Seattle Seahawks had a vicious defensive secondary known as "the Legion of Boom."

The Kansas City marketing machine loves to tout "Chief's Kingdom" as a moniker for its rabid fan base. It is harmless enough for the fans, but it illustrates an essential reason why discipleship is difficult. There are hundreds, maybe thousands, of rival kingdoms presented to us each day. There is the rival kingdom of success, which invites us to sacrifice everything else to achieve an ever-elusive measure of success. There is the rival kingdom of wealth, which, like success, invites us to surrender everything to gain more money. Its rallying cry is, "How much money is enough? Just a little bit more." There is the rival kingdom of power, which declares, "It doesn't matter who you must step on to gain another rung on the corporate ladder. Just do it!" Our politicians vie for our allegiance, promising that their platforms or programs will solve humanity's problems. Even education invites us to invest our lives in the pursuit of knowledge as if merely knowing the right answers will surely solve the problems of the world.

We find ourselves continually invited to give our allegiance to any number of these rival kingdoms. Akin to death by fingernail clippers, every interaction with these kingdoms seems to snip off a little piece of us until we discover we have little left.

All these rival kingdoms stand in stark contrast to Jesus and his teaching. It was Jesus, who in the context of rescuing his disciples from the pursuit of the tangible, but temporal, said, "But seek first his kingdom and his righteousness, and all these things will be given to you as well" (Matt. 6:33). It was also Jesus who said, "Enter through the narrow gate. For wide is the gate and broad is the road that leads to destruction, and many enter through it. But small is the gate and narrow the road that leads to life, and only a few find it" (7:13-14).

Jesus's kingdom must be our first allegiance. It's not wrong to cheer on your favorite sports team, have a well-paying job, know a measure of success, or be well educated. These things are a part of the human experience in our culture. But we cannot get confused about our primary allegiance. Jesus Christ saved us from a life of pain and eternal misery. He has offered us new life and a hope undimmed by circumstance through the power of his Spirit. Jesus showed us abundant life, died to bring it within our reach, and empowered us to make it possible. We have discovered this incredible gift, but it isn't enough to know it ourselves; we must pass it along to those in our circles of influence.

Discipleship isn't easy, but it is essential to the mission of God. Thankfully, God's amazing grace makes Jesus's commission attainable. John Wesley's ministry provides an essential concept that, once learned, activates our growth in Christ and unlocks our hidden capacity to become disciple makers. Wesley called it the *means of grace*. As the next chapter shows, the means of grace shaped early Methodism and offers us a practical way to grasp how God's purposes get carried out through the joint efforts of ordinary people like you and me.

five
THE MEANS OF GRACE
Activating God's Grace for God's Mission

A few years ago, my son and I were returning from a motorcycle trip in Utah. As usual we had ridden a little too long and had to hurry home. We loaded the bikes on the trailer and drove well into the night. I took the first leg of the journey while he rested, and then we switched so I could try to catch some sleep. I drifted off a bit and awoke to notice that the mileage readout in the SUV showed that we had about nine miles until we ran out of gas. The next gas station was about the same distance, according to the most recent highway sign. So we slowed our pace and prayed that the "miles to empty" computer had some wiggle room.

Unfortunately, the computer proved accurate, and we coasted to a stop about five miles from the exit. We unloaded one of the motorcycles, and I rode to the nearest gas station and returned with a brand-new gas can full of gas. However, we soon discovered, much to our dismay, that the spout on the gas can was broken. There was no way to pour the precious fuel into the tank of the SUV! We did finally get back on the road after my son customized an old water bottle for the task. It wasn't perfect; we spilled as much as we poured in the tank, but we made it to the exit and fueled up. Although everything turned out well, for a brief time we faced the frustration of knowing we had fuel but seemingly no way to put it to use.

So far we have established that God lavishes grace on us. He draws us, saves us, sanctifies us, and sustains us. We've also established that God bestows all that grace not just for our sake but for us to engage in the age-old mission of God. We've determined that it takes disciples of Jesus to carry out this mission but that both being and making disciples these days proves challenging. Like our faulty gas can full of fuel, God's grace is here and sufficient for the need, but we aren't sure how to access all that grace and apply it to the great need around us.

We aren't alone in this dilemma. Jesus's own disciples were paralyzed in their mission until the day of Pentecost. The indwelling Spirit of God set them free and birthed the church. But after the explosive growth of the church, as recounted in the book of Acts, the followers of Jesus have had hit-and-miss success with the Great Commission. Periods of effective discipleship have been followed by periods of struggle. We have already established the discipleship challenges of the church in postmodern America.

For this reason, it is vital to return to our guide from the past, John Wesley. We must rediscover Wesley's singular focus on holiness of heart and life *and* his practical application of the means of grace. A reawakening to Wesley's most defining channel of God's grace, the prudential means of grace, provides the pathway to discipleship renewal, as we will soon see.

The cause of spreading holiness throughout the land propelled John Wesley and laid the foundation for the Holiness Movement. This foundation stands strong, but we must discover or, in the case of the means of grace, rediscover a way to effectively build upon it. It is crucial for the church to find a way to capture the imaginations of its people and invite them into a grace-filled and responsive life of following Christ, pursuing the mission of God, and making disciples. In Wesley's own words:

> [People] are generally lost in the hurry of life, in the business or pleasures of it, and seem to think that their regeneration, their new nature, will spring and grow up within them, with as little care and thought of their own as their bodies were conceived and have attained their full strength and stature; whereas, there is nothing more certain than that the Holy Spirit will not purify our nature, unless we carefully attend to his motions, which are lost upon us while, in the Prophet's language, we "scatter away our time,"—while we squander away our thoughts upon

unnecessary things, and leave our spiritual improvement, the one thing needful, quite unthought of and neglected.[1]

Did you catch the phrase "unless we carefully attend to his motions"? Wesley is hinting at a crucial element in his theology, one that elsewhere he will refer to as the means of grace. Wesley believed and taught that though God has done the "heavy lifting" through grace, Christians are called to respond in obedience to that grace. Just ahead we'll take a deeper look at Wesley's means of grace, but for now, take heart: Jesus has not only called us to discipleship but made it possible as well.

One of the hallmarks of the holiness doctrine is its optimism. We doggedly insist that God is still able to transform lives from the inside out. What God can do for individuals, God can do for the church. By keeping an eye on both the theology and *methodology* of John Wesley, the church can answer Jesus's call to be and make disciples. Let's turn our attention to Wesley's foundational understanding of the means of grace.

The Origins of the Means of Grace for John Wesley

In the 1990s, Germany's largest chemical company, BASF, aired commercials in the United States. Their catchphrase was quite memorable. After reminding us that they didn't make blue jeans, but they did make them bluer; that they didn't make the airplane, but they did make it lighter; and so on, a smooth female voice would say, "At BASF we don't make a lot of the

---

1. John Wesley, Sermon 138, "On Grieving the Holy Spirit," in *Works of John Wesley*, ed. Jackson, 7:489.

products you buy; we make a lot of the products you buy better."[2] To understand John Wesley's use of the phrase "means of grace," we must begin by acknowledging that he didn't coin the term, but he did make it better.

Wesley inherited the phrase "means of grace" from the Puritan and Anglican traditions prevalent in his day. However, he did not work out his conception of the means of grace in the sterile environment of the academy, but rather his understanding was inspired by his parish work. Because he cherished his role as pastor, what Wesley believed and taught had to make sense to the everyday people in his ministry. In his own words, Wesley defined the means of grace: "By 'means of grace' I understand outward signs, words, or actions ordained of God, and appointed for this end—to be the *ordinary* channels whereby he might convey to men preventing, justifying, or sanctifying grace."[3]

Central to this definition is the phrase "ordinary channels." Wesley searched the Scriptures and the history of the church to discover how God had effectively worked. Though he was sometimes accused of it, Wesley wasn't searching for a novel approach to Christianity. Instead, he was interested in recovering what he felt had been lost along the way. Like a detective searching for clues, Wesley combed through the Bible

2. "BASF Ad from 1997—Making Everything Better," YouTube video, 0:30, posted by ClassicCommercials4U, October 25, 2009, https://www.youtube.com/watch?v=ZJHPpsb3FzM.

3. John Wesley, Sermon 16, "The Means of Grace," in *John Wesley's Sermons: An Anthology*, ed. Albert C. Outler and Richard P. Heitzenrater (Nashville: Abingdon Press, 1991), 160.

○ ○ ○

Whether it be awakening
a sinner to the need
for faith or forming
the believer into the
likeness of Christ, the
means of grace were the
channels through which
God's grace and human
response flowed.

○ ○ ○

and the history of the church for God's customary means of conveying grace to people.

The Value of the Means of Grace

Wesley understood the means of grace to be scriptural. In his message by the same title, he referenced Scripture repeatedly, quoting the Gospels, the writings of Paul, and the book of James. He declared that not only did the apostles avail themselves of the means of grace, but so did our Lord.[4] It is upon this foundation in Scripture that Wesley built his understanding and application of the means of grace.

Additionally, he understood the means of grace to be relational. By this Wesley intended to speak of the relationship between God and humanity. God desires that his creation live in relationship with God in the present. "Overall, the means of grace are really God's gifts to us. They are the ways we connect with God and participate in our relationship with him. As we open ourselves to God, God pours his own life and the grace we need into our hearts. When that happens, we will change; we will be spiritually formed and transformed."[5] It makes sense, then, that the means of grace are the practices that facilitate this life-changing relationship.

Wesley understood the means of grace to be essential. He was clear that the sole aim of the means was holiness of heart

---

4. Ibid., 161-62.

5. Diane Leclerc, "Finding the Means to the End: Christian Discipleship and Formation Practices," in *Spiritual Formation: A Wesleyan Paradigm*, ed. Diane Leclerc and Mark A. Maddix (Kansas City: Beacon Hill Press of Kansas City, 2011), 85.

and life, and without the solitary work of God this was impossible. Whether it be awakening a sinner to the need for faith or forming the believer into the likeness of Christ, the means of grace were the channels through which God's grace and human response flowed.[6] Without the means of grace, then, Wesley understood people to be staring helplessly across the chasm between God and humanity. It was the means of grace that opened a life-giving connection.

Importantly, Wesley saw the means of grace as communal. If we evaluate the means of grace, we find that each of them is more effectively practiced in community rather than alone. As indicated earlier, following Jesus works out best if we make the journey together. As we discover the various means of grace in the sections just ahead, consider them as conceivable in private practice but much more effective when practiced in cooperation with other believers.

Understanding the Means of Grace

The means of grace represented, as Wesley said, the ways that God works in the hearts and lives of people, through quite accessible channels, to bring about growth in grace. Importantly, however, believers must be active participants in that grace. Like every healthy relationship, the interactions go both ways.

When my wife and I began to date in college, she overwhelmed me with sweet expressions of affection. I'd find cookies in a little box on my car or a note tucked into my textbook.

---

6. Wesley, *Sermon 16*, "The Means of Grace," in *John Wesley's Sermons*, 162-63.

It wasn't long until I wanted to respond in kind. Not being as creative or clever, my kindnesses expressed to her were clumsy but well received. I imagine that had I paid little attention to her gestures, we wouldn't have dated for very long. Love expressed calls for a response. Out of a heart of love, God pours out grace and invites us to respond in constructive ways to that grace. Our responses to God's grace might be described as "graced practices." That is, Wesley believed that there were certain responses to grace that, when done repeatedly over time, enabled the transformation of the believer.[7] These means of grace take hold when in a kind of divine-human interplay, believers respond to the outpoured grace of God.

A pastor recently compared the means of grace to the giant, suspended bucket at a water park. Water is pumped up into the bucket until eventually the bucket tips over and all that water comes gushing down on the heads of delighted children. The pastor said that just as a child positions herself or himself under that gush of water, so should the believer in Jesus position herself or himself under the means of grace—those places where God has consistently poured out grace. God initiates the pouring out of grace, but our response is to position ourselves in the trajectory of that grace.

This is what we have been trying to find. This is the missing piece to the puzzle of God's generous grace and the daunt-

---

7. Aimee Stone Cooper, "Means of Grace as Formative Holiness: The Role and Significance of John Wesley's Spiritual Formation Practices in Pursuit of Christian Holiness for the Church of the Nazarene" (DMin diss., George Fox University, 2016), app. viii, 19-23.

ing responsibility to employ that grace in his mission. The means of grace unlocks the ability that enables us to pursue God's plans with success and empowers us to overcome the currents of culture that make discipleship so challenging.

The Various Means of Grace

While Wesley never created a definitive list of the means of grace, scholars have pored over his sermons, journal entries, letters, and meeting minutes to create a fluid list. Henry H. Knight's grouping seems to be the clearest approach. Knight lists three major categories for Wesley's means of grace.[8]

The General Means of Grace

The general means of grace is the broadest category for Wesley. While this category isn't specifically mentioned in Wesley's sermon on the means of grace, it is first referenced in the *Minutes* of the 1745 Methodist Conference:

Q. 11. How should we wait for the fulfilling of this promise [of entire sanctification]?

A. In universal obedience; in keeping all the commandments; in denying ourselves, and taking up our cross daily. These are the general means which God hath ordained for our receiving his sanctifying grace.[9]

---

8. Henry H. Knight III, *The Presence of God in the Christian Life: John Wesley and the Means of Grace* (Lanham, MD: Scarecrow Press, 1987), 5.

9. Andrew C. Thompson, "The General Means of Grace," *Methodist History* 51, no. 4 (July 2013), 250. Knight, drawing from other Wesley resources, rounds out this list by adding "watching" and "exercise of the presence of God." Knight, *Presence of God*, 5.

The general means of grace are less practices and more an awareness of "one's motivations in thought, word, and action . . . that collectively constitute a kind of faithful disposition toward all that one does in pursuit of sanctification."[10] In simpler terms, the general means of grace demonstrate our intent to be followers of Jesus. The saving grace of God moves us to choose obedience and self-denial. As the soil is to the flower, so are the general means the dispositions out of which the other means flourish.

The Instituted Means of Grace

This category is much easier to grasp for most believers. Wesley specifically mentioned three instituted means in his sermon on the means of grace. These were prayer, searching the Scriptures, and the Lord's Supper. However, in his later works he added both fasting and Christian conferencing. Wesley understood these activities to be appointed by God and universal to the church in all eras and cultures—thus, instituted. In the instituted means, Wesley believed that God had specifically ordained these practices to be conduits of grace. If we recall the water-park bucket analogy, when we pray, search the Scriptures, celebrate the Lord's Supper, fast, and meet in godly fellowship (Christian conferencing), we position ourselves under the flow of God's poured-out grace.

So we should pray. In Wesley's opinion, prayers should spring out of a sincere heart. While his Anglican training at first kept him focused on formal and written prayers, in time his pastoral practice opened the door to extemporaneous

---

10. Thompson, "General Means of Grace," 250.

prayers in several forms. Prayers should, from his perspective, contain petition, confession, intercession, and thanksgiving. Wesley loved the Anglican Book of Common Prayer, but in places where he found it difficult for the everyday Christian, he adapted it. To summarize, the style and format of prayer mattered less than the heart-to-heart communion between the Christian and God.[11]

Wesley also modeled searching the Scriptures as an essential means of grace in the life of the believer. The Scriptures provided the wellspring for his life and ministry and constituted an essential channel through which God could pour his sanctifying grace.[12] As a Christian leader, Wesley was at the same time well read and "a man of one book,"[13] employing the intelligence and education God had given him in the priority he gave to the Scriptures.

The Lord's Supper has been called the chief among Wesley's means of grace. Wesley believed that since Jesus had specifically instructed his followers to receive the Lord's Supper, it was incumbent upon believers to comply. He received the Lord's Supper at least weekly and admonished his Methodists to receive Communion as often as possible.[14] It was for him the food for the soul as a memorial to Christ's atoning work, the

---

11. Dean Gray Blevins, "John Wesley and the Means of Grace: An Approach to Christian Religious Education" (PhD diss., Claremont School of Theology, 1999), 181-85.

12. Ibid., 188-94.

13. John Wesley, preface to *Sermons on Several Occasions*, in *Works of John Wesley*, ed. Jackson, 5:3.

14. Cooper, "Means of Grace as Formative Holiness," 49-51.

real presence of Christ in the act of communing, and a promise of the coming glory. Wesley believed that God's grace flowed freely through the bread and cup.

Wesley believed in and practiced fasting as a means of grace. He believed that abstinence from food was a worthwhile practice, since it opened more time for prayer and defeated the grip of temporal things on us, reminding us of our dependence upon God.

His views on Christian conferencing are insightful as well. For Wesley, conferencing might include gatherings for fellowship and instruction as we might more traditionally define a conference. But Wesley also held that "rightly ordered conversations" that offered channels of God's grace to believers were a means of grace.[15] This perspective on the value of Christian discourse not only is well rounded but also speaks across the years and is, like its counterparts, applicable today.

Remember the makeshift funnel my son made to get the gasoline into our SUV? John Wesley understood the instituted means of grace to be that funnel through which God poured out sanctifying grace. These five activities resonate with us as we practice our faith, but don't miss the point. God is acting in grace, but we have a role to play as well. Like the little girl with the Mother's Day flower in chapter 1, we are participating with God in our growth. God is certainly doing the heavy lifting, but we are also doing our part as we take full advantage of the instituted means of grace.

---

15. Knight, *Presence of God*, 5.

The Prudential Means of Grace

Kansas City is famous for barbecue. Every city, town, or village has at least one and often several barbecue restaurants. All of them have brisket, pulled pork, ribs, and a variety of house-made sauces. You would think that the hungry folks of Kansas City might quickly tire of these options, but they don't. What I learned after moving here eight years ago is that although every restaurant has similar menu options, each shop is unique in some way. I now have my favorite haunts for brisket, a different place for burnt ends, and a sauce or two that I buy by the bottle.

Wesley's instituted means of grace seem like standard items on the Christian "menu." We all understand these actions to be what the people of God do. But what makes Wesley unique and what made Methodism so powerful in eighteenth-century England was Wesley's understanding of what he called the *prudential* means of grace.

In the Larger Minutes of 1778, Wesley introduced the concept of the prudential means of grace.[16] Henry H. Knight identifies the prudential means of grace as follows:

1. Particular rules or acts of holy living.
2. Class and band meetings.
3. Prayer meetings, covenant services, watch night services, love feasts.
4. Visiting the sick.
5. Doing all the good one can, doing no harm.

---

16. Blevins, "John Wesley and the Means of Grace," 173.

    6. Reading devotional classics and all edifying literature.[17]

A quick explanation might help us understand these a bit better. Wesley realized that when Christians did the things that Christians do, they grew in their relationship with Christ. He quickly discovered that God could work in ways that he hadn't categorized as instituted means of grace. For instance, when Wesley gathered his converts into smaller groups for prayer and discipleship, he discovered that God richly blessed those gatherings. When his designated leaders visited the sick to pray with them, they returned to report that not only had God helped the sick, but also the leaders themselves felt as though they had grown. Wesley was an avid reader, not only maintaining a personal library but also personally funding the reprints of several works he felt would be edifying to his pastors and leaders. In the reading of devotional works Wesley understood that God could work powerfully.

Eventually, Wesley would refer to these prudential means as "arts of holy living,"[18] capturing a sense of the beautiful ways that God could work through these responses to grace. Importantly for us, Wesley was always open to discover new ways that God was pouring out grace and he was quick to adapt time-honored practices to make them even more effective.

In fact, the very things that distinguished the early Methodist "menu" from that of the Anglicans and other movements

---

17. Knight, *Presence of God*, 5.

18. Kenneth J. Collins, "John Wesley and the Means of Grace," *The Drew Gateway* 56, no. 3 (Spring 1986): 27.

○ ○ ○

The prudential means
of grace were the
reasons for Methodism's
rapid growth and
effectiveness in
changing not just
the church but the
nation as well.

○ ○ ○

were Wesley's prudential means. The class meeting is a terrific example. It was these small group gatherings that provided the setting for loving accountability and kept the early Methodists on the path of holiness. These prudential means of grace were the reasons for Methodism's rapid growth and effectiveness in changing not just the church but the nation as well. Further, it will be in the spirit of the prudential means of grace that we find a foundation for discipleship renewal in the days to come.

The Origins of the Prudential Means

I enjoy baseball, basketball, and football more than any other sports. I like my car to be clean and to operate well. I am no stranger to casseroles and fried chicken. I value education and church attendance. I can understand if that list seems random to you, but it illustrates an important component of the means of grace and John Wesley. The things I listed above are all a part of my unique experience. My dad liked traditional sports and cars. My mom was a terrific Midwestern cook, and she and Dad made sure I was in church and made good grades. I am, to this day, very much a product of my environment. The same is true of John Wesley and his defining concept of the means of grace.

Wesley's home life and education were significant factors in his development of the prudential means of grace. While his father may have favored classical theology, his mother was left with the task of raising children who would know and serve God. No doubt Susanna's Puritan heritage steeped her in prudence, and before her children could articulate it, Susanna Wesley was modeling the prudential means of grace in her interactions with them. She wanted to see her children love and serve God and was motivated to find the means to this end. It is enlightening to read snippets of her correspondence with her children as they left home for their education. Clearly, she expected them to continue in her methods, and for the most part they appear to have consented.[19] Her strict routines, her weekly meetings with each child, and her insistence on the primacy of Scripture and prayer, all done within the context of eighteenth-century English homelife, were expressions of what Wesley would later practice as prudential means of grace.

Additionally, John Wesley was influenced by the education he received in the spirit of the day in which he lived. Wesley was well read in philosophy, empiricism, and Platonism. It was inevitable that the popular trends in learning would influence the development of his ministry.

We are all influenced by our heritage and environment to some degree, but Wesley kept this in balance with his absolute passion for holiness of heart and life. In his *Thoughts upon Methodism*, Wesley wrote, "From this short sketch of Methodism (so called,) any man of understanding may easily discern, that it is only plain, scriptural religion, guarded by a few prudential regulations. The essence of it is holiness of heart and life; the circumstantials all point to this."[20]

---

19. D. Michael Henderson, *John Wesley's Class Meeting: A Model for Making Disciples* (Nappanee, IN: Evangel, 1997), 39.

20. John Wesley, *Thoughts upon Methodism*, in *Works of John Wesley*, ed. Jackson, 13:260.

God used Wesley's keen mind, Puritan work ethic, era in human history, and organizational skill to bring about a revival of holiness in England. Is it possible that by prayerfully learning from his example that we might see spiritual renewal in our day as well?

Kenneth Collins, noted Wesleyan scholar, thinks so:

Positively, the prudential means of grace provide the structure, the parameters, through which the greatest advances in grace can be realized in Christian practice. In other words, prudential means are those which are considered prudent by an enlightened reason and by informed experience and which direct and guide the spiritual life as it continues to encounter the rich grace of God both in and through these particular practices. Wesley called them "arts of holy living."[21]

Many of the developments that later proved key to the success of Methodism, such as the class meeting, the penny collection, and the watch-night services, were driven by reason and necessity and became prudential means of God's grace. Over and again in *A Plain Account of the People Called Methodists* one can see the prudent and practical side of Wesley. Perhaps most telling are these words: "The Scripture, in most points, gives only general rules; and leaves the particular circumstances to be adjusted by the common sense of mankind. . . . That is, they are methods which men have found, by reason and

---

21. Collins, "John Wesley and the Means of Grace," 27.

common sense, for the more effectually applying several Scripture rules, couched in general terms, to particular occasions."[22]

It is clear, then, that as John Wesley applied himself to the cause of holiness of heart and life, he drew from his experience and environment to adopt those practices that would be channels through which God could pour grace. These pious and reasoned practices Wesley termed the prudential means of grace.

The Interdependence of the Means of Grace

It seems that most of the people in my family love bread. We can't explain it scientifically, so perhaps it is a function of our Midwestern upbringing, but we love bread. I also love peanut butter. You can probably see where this is heading. Sometimes I just crave a good old peanut butter and jelly sandwich. If the bread is supersoft, so much the better. By themselves, each ingredient of a PB and J sandwich is good, but together, they are magical. I don't think John Wesley ever had a PB and J, but I know he understood the benefit of the various means of grace working together in the life of the believer.

Wesley believed that while our salvation has a beginning point, a gradual process growing "out of our responsive participation in God's forgiving and empowering grace" often marks the pathway to holiness.[23] For Wesley, the means of grace

---

22. John Wesley, *A Plain Account of the People Called Methodists*, in *Works of John Wesley*, ed. Jackson, 8:255.

23. Randy L. Maddox, *Responsible Grace: John Wesley's Practical Theology* (Nashville: Kingswood Books, 1994), 192.

enabled that "responsive participation." The grace of God is conveyed to the believer through the means, and the faithful response of the believer is conveyed back to God.

Indeed, the goal of the Christian, for Wesley, was holiness of heart and life. Although he wasn't systematic in his approach to the means of grace, offering a checklist of sorts, he was directive, instructing his Methodists in the vital importance of utilizing all the means of grace for Christian living.

The instituted means of grace of the Church of England were vulnerable. "People could come to them again and again without experiencing the [life-transforming] presence of God. What was needed were other means of grace which would nurture faith through encouraging a receptive and expectant openness to God, and a faithful and loving response."[24] Seeing that from time to time the traditional means of grace in the Church of England grew routine and ceased to present occasions for spiritual progress, Wesley offered the prudential means to achieve these ends.

Considering this, one of the most important aspects of Wesley's means of grace is that they operate best when they operate together. Remember the PB and J sandwich? For Wesley, there was no either-or approach to the means of grace. For him, it was always a both-and proposition. One can picture the eighteenth-century Methodists faithfully attending the Church of England: hearing sermons, participating in the Lord's Supper, and experiencing the liturgy. But one can also envision them

---

24. Knight, *Presence of God*, 35.

attending a society meeting: gathering for accountability, godly counsel, faithful instruction, hymn singing, testimonies, and prayer. For Wesley, both were essential to the pursuit of holiness of heart and life and evident in his own personal practice.

The hallmarks of the Methodist movement—societies, class meetings, bands, covenant services, conferencing, and love feasts—were all made possible because Wesley saw them as channels through which God's grace could flow. Without this interdependence, the ongoing influence of Wesley and the Methodists would have disappeared long ago.[25]

Without question, John Wesley was an orthodox theologian and thoroughly grounded in the Anglicanism of his day. Wesley was also a realist. As his ministry increasingly spread from the academy to the coal yards, Wesley developed a more robust understanding of the means of grace. While he never rejected the instituted means, he understood and taught that God's sanctifying grace was conveyed through more than just the rituals of the Church of England. Wesley adapted a wide variety of concepts and practices that not only rounded out his theology but more importantly made him highly effective in his pastoral ministry.

The Means of Grace Today

Wesley was eager to present the world a fresh perspective on grace, but we must never attempt to simply replicate Wesley's means of grace in the modern day. A better alternative is to

---

25. Blevins, "John Wesley and the Means of Grace," 227, 350-51.

understand the spirit behind Wesley's means of grace and make fresh applications in current circumstances.[26] This appears to swing wide the door for pastors and leaders in the twenty-first century to carefully explore creative avenues for God's grace to be poured out on believers in pursuit of sanctification and to enable these disciples of Jesus to effectively disciple others.

Similarly, the means of grace, in particular the prudential means, are best imagined as ways to engage people at the point of their need. The shear complexity of human need surely calls for the church to enlist its entire creative prowess under the direction of the Holy Spirit to teach believers that God's grace is available.[27] Wesley didn't see grace confined to the practices of the official church but certainly adopted and adapted new practices to urge people forward in the pursuit of holiness of heart and life. This approach recaptures the Spirit of Wesley for the modern day.

The Means of Grace in John Wesley's Practice

Perhaps this idea of adoption and adaption is best seen by looking to Wesley himself. One can observe in Wesley a dynamic relationship with the various means of grace as God blessed them and Christians were nurtured.

Though reluctant at first, Wesley eventually appreciated the value of extemporaneous prayer when coupled with the more formal prayers of the church. As time passed, Wesley also

---

26. Knight, *Presence of God*, 5, 15, 48.
27. Blevins, "John Wesley and the Means of Grace," 209-10.

permitted the society meetings to evolve more into worship services as the people became more and more reluctant to attend the services of the Church of England. His reluctant use of lay preachers represents a significant departure from the formalized ordination processes of the Church of England. He also adapted the Christian calendar, removing several of the holy days that seemed a distraction to his people. He further introduced the singing of hymns as an innovation over the metrical psalms regularly used by the formal church.

Wesley adopted and adapted the Moravian love feast for the use of his Methodists. In addition, he adapted the watchnight service and the covenant services to Methodist practice. The entire organization of societies, classes, and bands represents a foundational means of grace for Wesley, as did Christian conferencing.

From the Puritans and the long tradition of the wider church, Wesley adapted his class meetings into a form of catechumenate for the Methodists. It was here that seekers were able to learn the foundations of the faith. Even things considered sacraments in other traditions, such as foot washing, were eventually seen by Wesley as means of grace.

It's clear that adaptation was an essential methodology for Wesley.[28] Once again, it appears that Rev. Wesley offers modern pastors and leaders opportunities for the creative application of the means of grace.

---

28. Maddox, *Responsible Grace*, 205-19.

Further Implications of the Prudential Means for Discipleship Renewal

Wesley's prudential means of grace offer a framework in which the modern church can work. The church can embrace, as Wesley did, creative and practical expressions of the faith.

In the spirit of Wesley, then, believers can begin to think creatively about discipleship. While innovation for its own sake or for the sake of attracting a crowd falls short of true discipleship, innovation embraced for its ability to lead to discipleship is an authentically Wesleyan approach. By recapturing a distinctively Wesleyan discipleship model, heart change and life transformation can become a more frequent reality. Many are arguing for various reforms in the church in these days, but reforms in the methodology of discipleship and in the spirit of Wesley's Methodists seem a proven way forward.

We began this chapter reliving a time when my son and I ran out of gas. Let's go back there for just a moment to link that experience to a specific Wesleyan discipleship plan we will explore in chapter 6.

When we coasted to a stop beside the interstate, I didn't have a problem, *we* had a problem. *We* set about to figure it out. I initially proposed that I could walk or jog ahead to the nearest station and bring back some fuel. It was my son who quickly reminded me that we had two fueled-up motorcycles at our disposal. One could be unloaded and driven to the nearest station. Once there, a friendly clerk helped me locate what I needed and complete my purchase. When I returned, my son and I together completed the sloppy task of refueling through our makeshift funnel. Our rescue was a *team effort*. All of us working together—father, son, and clerk—made the refueling possible.

As we conceive a way forward for discipleship, John Wesley and the example of the early Methodists taught us that trying to take on the mission of God alone is not likely to work. The effort to be a disciple and make disciples in obedience to Jesus's Great Commission is best undertaken in a truly Wesleyan fashion—in a small group built on loving accountability. Let's look at a proposed solution that capitalizes on the outpoured grace of God, takes seriously the mission of God, and, through the means of grace, develops disciples who are passionate about making disciples.

six
THE PRACTICAL GRACE
OF A
COVENANT GROUP
Loving Accountability in Action

I played basketball in college. Our coach preached teamwork, and we bought in. Many times, we beat teams with much better players because we had learned the importance of working together. If you've ever played college sports, you know that both your successes and failures are on full display. There is no place to hide when you compete, and a sense of personal responsibility for the team's successes and failures develops quickly. Our victories were sweeter as we celebrated team wins. When we lost, each of us felt responsible and worked hard to improve.

I've participated in many teams throughout the years, but none of them compares to that college experience. To this day, I still have dreams about playing with those guys and I cherish them. I did not know then that God had permitted me to learn the power of loving accountability. The bonds of love developed through shared experiences and the sense of responsibility for the success of the team were glimpses of what John Wesley would one day cultivate among his Methodists.

Wesley's desire to guide people into holiness of heart and life kept him busily adjusting his methods until he could find a practical and effective way forward. "Wesley's theological understanding . . . led him to adopt what first seemed an unbelievably straightforward solution: a weekly meeting of like-minded persons who would exercise a mutual accountability for their discipleship."[1] A key component of Wesley's Methodists that sums up this research is an expression of accountable discipleship termed "covenant discipleship."[2] Wesley's *A Plain Account of the People Called Methodists* summarizes what would eventually become a hallmark of Methodism: "They therefore united themselves 'in order to pray together, to receive the word of exhortation, and to watch over one another in love, that they might help each other to work out their salvation.'"[3] John Wesley brought together a lifetime of influences and experiences to discover a concept essential to holiness of heart and life.

This morning, I grinned as I watched my wife make a list detailing the food she would prepare for our holiday feast. She lives her life with careful organization and a host of checklists.

---

1. Watson, *Covenant Discipleship*, 38.

2. See Watson, *Accountable Discipleship*. Watson introduces the term "covenant discipleship" in the preface and then carries it throughout the book.

3. Wesley, *Plain Account of the People Called Methodists*, in *Works of John Wesley*, ed. Jackson, 8:250.

I grinned this morning because I've seen her mother do the very same thing. My mother-in-law taught her daughter to organize her life and that a pen-and-paper list is hard to beat for the task. John Wesley had a simple yet organized approach to discipleship, and he came by it honestly.

Susanna Wesley's careful discipleship with John and his siblings blended love and accountability into a pleasant encounter that was "warm and intimate sharing concerning the reality of God and the greatness of his provision and the joys of the Christian life."[4] These weekly sessions with his mother created the furrows in the mind of young John where the seeds of group accountability would one day germinate.

The involvement of Samuel Wesley, John's father, in the early English religious societies taught John the importance of gathering for encouragement and accountability with a small group of like-minded believers, and John joined the Society for Promoting Christian Knowledge in 1732. These societies were eighteenth-century English expressions of German Pietism's "'little church' in the 'big church.'"[5] These influences shaped the early academic career of Wesley and his formation of the Holy Club at Oxford. This early expression of a small group under Wesley's leadership was a forerunner of future expressions of accountable discipleship.

Wesley's mission to America gave him a further laboratory in which to test his evolving methodology. His efforts were met with varying degrees of success, but the voyage back to

---

4. Henderson, *John Wesley's Class Meeting*, 38.
5. Watson, *Covenant Discipleship*, 23-28.

England would expose Wesley to the Moravians, whose simple faith and practical group organization would lead not only to his Aldersgate experience[6] but also to his initial efforts in Methodist classes and bands.[7] Wesley's passion for holiness motivated him to adapt effective methods he encountered in order to provide a system for watching over the spiritual development of the early Methodists.

These classes and bands, or smaller classes, were built around a methodological component that is largely missing from our churches in the postmodern era. At the very core of the success of the Methodist revival was John Wesley's insistence on accountability. It was Wesley who, after preaching, gathered together those who had been awakened and organized them into smaller groups where there would be an ongoing sense of accountability for spiritual progress toward holiness. It is precisely this accountability that made spiritual awakenings stick and grow into holiness of heart and life. It is this accountability that will provide a loving environment for discipleship renewal in our churches.

---

6. This pivotal experience for John Wesley happened on May 24, 1738, when Wesley felt his "heart strangely warmed" while attending a society meeting in Aldersgate Street at the reading of Martin Luther's *Preface to the Epistle to the Romans.* Wesley interpreted this experience as an assurance of his trust in Christ and of his salvation from sin and death. John Wesley, Journal entry for May 24, 1738, in *Works of John Wesley,* ed. Jackson, 1:103.

7. Henderson, *John Wesley's Class Meeting,* 44-58.

The Early Methodist Class Meeting

The class meeting was the most influential instructional unit in Methodism and probably Wesley's greatest contribution to the church. The class meeting also provided the setting for accountable spiritual growth for the Methodists. Henry Ward Beecher said, "The greatest thing John Wesley ever gave to the world is the Methodist class meeting." Nineteenth-century evangelist Dwight L. Moody observed that "Methodist class meetings are the best institutions for training young converts the world ever saw."[8] It was in the class meeting that Wesley was able to finally fulfill his heart's desire to help people make progress in the pursuit of holiness. The tutelage of Wesley's homelife, his experiences in America, and the successes of the Oxford Holy Club contributed to a format that would permeate the lives of those desiring God and bring about in them lasting change. It was through the class meetings that Wesley believed his followers were closest to the practices of first-century Christians and tapping into the roots of primitive Christianity.

The Origins of the Class Meeting

A quick Google search will reveal that the pacemaker, potato chips, Silly Putty and the microwave oven all came into being through happy accidents. None of these products was the target, but in the effort to produce something else, these now

---

8. Charles L. Goodell, *The Drillmaster of Methodism: Principles and Methods for the Class Leader and Pastor* (New York: Eaton and Mains, 1902), 15, Internet Archive, https://archive.org/details/drillmasterofmet00good/page/14/mode/2up.

essential products were discovered. Similarly, John Wesley actually stumbled into his best methodology by accident.

In an effort to retire the debt of the society in Bristol, the idea was adopted to have a weekly penny collection from every member of the society. Once instituted, something surprising began to happen. Those who were visited in the collection of the offering soon began to share about the condition of their souls. Wesley took note of this and discovered the means of accountability that would mark Methodism for all time: "'This is the thing; the very thing we have wanted so long.' I called together all the Leaders of the classes, (so we used to term them and their companies,) and desired, that each would make a particular inquiry into the behaviour of those whom he saw weekly. . . . As soon as possible, the same method was used in London and all other places."[9] Thus began the early Methodist class meeting.

Specifically, accountability by way of the early classes was handled in the following manner:

> That it may the more easily be discerned, whether they are indeed working out their own salvation, each society is divided into smaller companies called *classes*, according to their respective places of abode. There are about twelve persons in every class; one of whom is styled *the Leader*. It is his business, (1.) To see each person in his class once a week at least, in order to inquire how their souls prosper; to advise, reprove, comfort, or exhort, as occasion may

---

9. Wesley, *Plain Account of the People Called Methodists*, in *Works of John Wesley*, ed. Jackson, 8:252-53.

require; to receive what they are willing to give toward the relief of the poor.[10]

Before very long the idea of visiting each member of a society in person became impractical, and the society members were invited to a weekly gathering. In time, these meetings became a weekly means of accountability as the participants gave not only an offering of money but also an offering of transparent accountability for the condition of their souls. Initially, the groups met wherever they could gather with ten or twelve members: schools, shops, attics, and even coalbins. Later, however, as the movement grew, Methodist chapels were constructed to house the class meetings in locations more convenient to the members.

The format was surprisingly simple and effective. After beginning precisely on the hour, a hymn was sung and the leader began by giving a short testimony on the condition of his or her soul. The leader's role was crucial because it set the tone for the vulnerability of the rest of the group. Open sharing about the successes and failures of the leader invited similar vulnerability in the members. Importantly, the class meetings were not designed for doctrinal ideology or scriptural instruction. The order of the day was personal experiences in walking out the pursuit of holiness. This created an informal but highly effective leveling among the members, engendering a spirit of nurture and collegiality.

---

10. John Wesley, *The Nature, Design, and General Rules of the United Societies, in London, Bristol, Kingswood, Newcastle-upon-Tyne,* in *Works of John Wesley,* ed. Jackson, 8:269-70.

The Class Meeting in Wesley's Organizational System

Wesley's reluctance to part with the Church of England meant that Methodism would not, at least during his lifetime, become a substitute for the church. Wesley considered his Methodists to be the "little church" within the "big church."[11] The various meetings of the Methodists were carefully scheduled to avoid conflict with the services of the Church of England. Wesley's intentions were not to compete with the church but rather to provide a component missing from the larger church—namely, a vehicle for the pursuit of holiness of heart and life. His accountability groups or class meetings provided this component.

The different parts of Wesley's Methodist system were set by 1742. There would be small adjustments along the way, but for the most part, the die was cast. The first category of the system was the society. The society was intended to include all the Methodists in a given locale. The society was the umbrella category for all of Methodism. "The primary function of the society was cognitive instruction: it was the educational channel by which the tenets of Methodism were presented to the target population."[12] Since merely education seldom leads to transformation, Wesley continued to refine his discipleship process.

Chronologically, the next category Wesley created were the bands. His idea was straightforward; people would be grouped together and taken through a series of questions. The questions pulled no punches:

---

11. Watson, *Covenant Discipleship*, 24.
12. Henderson, *John Wesley's Class Meeting*, 84.

○ ○ ○

The class meeting was precisely the instrument that Wesley sought. It was stringent enough to engage and challenge the new Methodists, yet not so advanced as to overwhelm them.

- "Have you peace with God, through our Lord Jesus Christ?"
- "Is the love of God shed abroad in your heart?"
- "Do you desire to be told of your faults?"
- "Do you desire that every one of us should tell you, from time to time, whatsoever is in his heart concerning you?"
- "Do you desire that, in doing this, we should come as close as possible, that we should cut to the quick, and search your heart to the bottom?"[13]

At least two things seem obvious from this line of questioning. The first is a glimpse into Wesley's upbringing and perhaps what it would have been like in the Holy Club. The second is that this intensity, especially for the newly converted, was a case of "too much too soon."[14] Ordinary working-class converts were not yet ready to deepen their faith in this way. They were simply trying to hold on to what faith they already had.[15] Wesley loved this category, and it would remain in Methodism, but something else was needed between the society and the band.

As detailed above, the class meeting was precisely the instrument that Wesley sought. It was stringent enough to engage and challenge the new Methodists, yet not so advanced as to overwhelm them. Additionally, the accountability was transferred to the group, which inevitably governed the intensity

13. John Wesley, "Rules of the Band-Societies," in *Works of John Wesley*, ed. Jackson, 8:272-73.

14. Watson, *Covenant Discipleship*, 30.

15. Ibid.

of the interactions initially and enabled the group to progress together.

This category Wesley would term "that excellent institution." He likened it to the "sinews" that hold together the human body, and as a result, the class meeting was the very muscle of the Methodist movement.[16] Wesley intuited that he had found the means to the desired goal of holiness. He would champion the class meeting and its emphases on accountability until his death.

This chapter began with a description of the bonds of teamwork and the accountability they provide. Thinking back to the introduction and the Apollo 11 mission, there is no way for me to know the inner workings of the Apollo 11 team, but I did observe in the film *Hidden Figures* the loving relationships and accountability that existed between the West Computers. The women loved each other, watched over each other, and together changed the world. I believe that kind of loving accountability is the prescription for a discipleship renewal in our churches.

How Wesley's Class Meeting Reflects a Prudential Means of Grace

The class meeting was the most widely practiced and effective expression of John Wesley's conviction that the church should imitate the practices of the earliest Christians. The genesis of Wesley's methodology was in the Scriptures. He under-

---

16. John Telford, ed., *The Letters of John Wesley* (London: Epworth Press, 1931), 4:194.

stood his preaching and teaching to be driving the Methodists back to the teachings of Jesus and the apostles.[17] Wesley instructed his Methodists to give themselves to the instituted means of grace, but to also engage in the prudential means of grace. Perhaps more important than any of the other identified prudential means of Methodism was Wesley's insistence on a small group structure for training converts. In the class meeting, Wesley understood his Methodists to be recovering the faith of the early church.

The various strata for discipleship developed by Wesley were all born of necessity. With his singular focus on holiness of heart and life, and in view of the ineffectiveness of the church in his day to produce it, Wesley found ways to engage people that led to real-life transformation. In his sermon "Causes of the Inefficacy of Christianity," a mature Wesley bemoaned the lack of real Christians in his day.[18] He understood his approach of gathering together in loving accountability those who were desperate "to flee the wrath to come"[19] to be a reasoned response to the situation at hand. By the occasion of this sermon, Wesley had had many years to observe the impact of his structure and its effectiveness. It was a practical response to be sure, but it was also clearly a necessary one. In order to attain

17. Albert C. Outler, ed., *The Works of John Wesley*, vols. 1-4, *The Sermons* (Nashville: Abingdon Press, 1986), 3:511; quoted in Kevin M. Watson, "The Form and Power of Godliness: Wesleyan Communal Discipline as Voluntary Suffering," *Wesleyan Theological Journal* 43, no. 1 (Spring 2008): 166.

18. John Wesley, Sermon 122, "Causes of the Inefficacy of Christianity," in *John Wesley's Sermons*, 550-57.

19. Wesley, *Nature, Design, and General Rules*, in *Works of John Wesley*, ed. Jackson, 8:270.

the goal of holiness, Wesley acted upon his understanding of the means of grace to create the environment to enable it. The class meeting, with its insistence upon loving accountability, was that environment.

Recent Efforts in the Methodist Movement

There has been no shortage of calls for those who have inherited the Wesleyan tradition to return to the roots of the class and band structure. L. Gregory Jones offers a helpful phrase as we think about how to borrow Wesley's genius for the twenty-first century. The phrase is "traditioned innovation." Jones suggests that we can honor and engage the past while adapting to the future. In traditioned innovation we are invited to consider who we have been and who we will be in the face of an ever-changing cultural landscape.[20] The best way forward for the church in answering Jesus's call to be and make disciples is the route that John Wesley employed in the eighteenth century, which was not only paying attention to the current need but also exploring the vitality of Christian belief and practice across the centuries. We're still rowing the boat, aren't we? We are looking back to Wesley but straining toward a better future for discipleship in our churches.

Summing up the importance of group accountability to Wesley's approach to discipleship, Randy Maddox observes,

> One of Wesley's most central pastoral convictions was that authentic spiritual formation cannot take place "without

---

20. L. Gregory Jones, *Christian Social Innovation: Renewing Wesleyan Witness* (Nashville: Abingdon Press, 2016), 49.

society, without living and conversing with [others]." This is what led Wesley to create corporate structures to provide his Methodist people with mutual support for their spiritual journey. The most basic structure was the class meeting, and one of its central values was the balance of encouragement and accountability it provided.[21]

It's true that many of Wesley's theological descendants have moved away from an emphasis on loving accountability. However, I believe the time is right for those of us who stand in the shadow of John Wesley to take up the cause.

Key and Transferable Components of the Class Meeting to a Modern Church Setting

Making application of these concepts to our churches must begin with noting that John Wesley and his theological descendants share a common target—helping people grow in holiness. Nothing was more central to Wesley's goals than to overcome the nominal faith of his day. This is still the clear goal for our churches now. Key to any recovery of the methodology of Wesley will mean cultivating a biblically grounded and theologically balanced sense of what it means to be a real disciple. Accountable discipleship is aimed primarily at this target, and the class meeting was the environment where Wesley saw it happen. There is a genuine hunger in the lives of church attendees to make progress in holiness. By a traditioned inno-

---

21. Randy L. Maddox, "Wesley's Prescription for 'Making Disciples of Jesus Christ': Insights for the Twenty-First-Century Church," *Quarterly Review* 23, no. 1 (Spring 2003): 27.

vation of the underlying principles of the early Methodist class meeting, this hunger can be addressed.

To this end, a fresh re-presentation of the principles of the class meeting provides a tangible expression of the means of grace as Wesley understood and taught them. The presentation of a refreshed expression of accountable discipleship will demonstrate actual growth in grace. Accountable discipleship works because it trains the participant, through grace, to be more like Christ. Just as an athlete submits to repetition and hard work to achieve mastery, so does the Christian grow in holiness when she or he practices the disciplines of accountable discipleship.

Similarly, we can benefit from the traditioned innovation of the class meeting because the focus is less on teaching style and biblical expertise and more on the practice of living together by covenant. This approach will be new to most congregations. Sunday school and small group ministries today fall into the respective ditches of either lecture-based instruction or surface-level sharing about common concerns. The class meeting centers around a new approach of holding one another accountable to previously agreed-upon expressions of the means of grace. Group members, having been introduced to the principles of Wesley and the means of grace, meet together around a covenant they have created and, in a question-and-answer format, "watch over one another in love" to ensure that each member is living into the agreement formed by the group.

Likewise, these groups will model two things largely missing from postmodern churches—vulnerability and accountability. In the refreshed class meeting model, the leader goes first in honestly relating her or his successes and failures in living into the agreed-upon covenant. In so doing, the leader is modeling the means of relating for the rest of the group. The early Methodist class meeting demonstrated the power of this simple approach. As Christians openly shared in an environment built around the expectation that the covenant would be upheld, life transformation took place. This can be recaptured in our churches today.

There are a host of other important principles of the early Methodist class meeting that can be translated into today's settings. For one thing, since Wesley's groups were usually divided up by geography, they were not specifically linked to age. While certainly set up for adults, there was an element of intergenerational participation that could be recovered in churches today. Church people could benefit from this intergenerational approach to adult discipleship.

Women were also key leaders in the early Methodist classes. Consider how important this emphasis would be if churches fully embraced accountable discipleship groups led by both women and men. This model also lends itself to repeatability. The nature of the covenant-based group is less dependent on the personality of the leader or the specific makeup of the members. Instead, the emphasis is on the faithful following of the agreed-upon covenant. Nearly anyone can lead and still realize the effectiveness of the methodology. For similar reasons, this makes the accountable discipleship model accessible to any congregation whose attendees are serious about the pursuit of holiness.

○ ○ ○

People who share from
their hearts regularly
develop strong ties
to one another and to
their common goals for
spiritual growth.

Inevitably, while not the only goal, the covenant-based discipleship model does foster strong connections between its members. People who share from their hearts regularly develop strong ties to one another and to their common goals for spiritual growth. This depth of relationship will only help the church.

Lastly, the early Methodist class meeting became the first level of leadership training for the movement. Class leaders who proved faithful and effective often became a part of Wesley's greater leadership structure. How essential for the renewal of the church to be led by people who are serious in their pursuit of holiness. A pastor could, in time, realize an entirely new group of leaders based not on popularity or longevity but on participation in the transformational practices of accountable discipleship.

A Contemporary Model of Accountable Discipleship

Accountability like this must be a part of any efforts toward true discipleship renewal within our churches. While worship services are essential, even from a Wesleyan perspective, they offer very little accountability. Small groups offer places to connect with others and share life experiences in the context of Christian fellowship, but precious few offer any accountable expectations that the members will make tangible progress toward holiness. Even the Sunday school, with its classic interest in biblical instruction, lacks a strong sense of accountability in the postmodern world.

We need a refreshed model of discipleship to re-form our fledgling disciples in the essential importance of accountability that leads to life transformation. While perhaps a new expression of discipleship within our churches, this emphasis on accountability should not come as a surprise. No one would argue with the effectiveness of the Alcoholics Anonymous groups or Saddleback Church's Celebrate Recovery. Both highly effective programs have accountability to others as a centerpiece. Similarly, people regularly adopt Weight Watchers or other weight-loss programs that require accountability through weekly weigh-ins and input from a coach. Likewise, CrossFit and other similar movements require participants to join a group, show up to workouts, and pay a fee—all to help them achieve their fitness goals. People seem to have discovered the benefits of supportive accountability. What these relatively recent movements hold to be of critical importance was figured out long ago in Methodism's groups—namely, that supportive accountability leads to lasting change.

The American Society of Training and Development (ASTD) recently completed a study on accountability. The ASTD discovered that if an individual commits to another person for the completion of a goal, that individual has a 65 percent chance of completing the goal. However, that percentage jumps to 95 percent if that commitment is coupled with a "specific accountability appointment." According to the study, the most challenging goals can be successfully achieved if a person commits to regular accountability.[22] I came across this research in a conversation with a life coach who I hired to help me develop a plan to write the book you are holding. In our discussions it became clear that writing a book about accountability while I myself was a part of an accountable relationship made perfect sense. My coach and I established Tuesday mornings at 9:00 a.m. for a Zoom call, we set some measurable goals, and we began our work. I was astonished that as the days turned into weeks, I was not only hitting my targets but was actually ahead of schedule. I felt a little like the Apollo 11 team. Kennedy gave them a deadline, and they finished well before it. Verifiable evidence exists that accountability works. You are reading it![23]

This book means to leverage this reality for the cause of discipleship. I propose a six-week small group experience designed to hold participants accountable to the message of holiness as it contrasts with the counter-formational messages of our culture. The six weeks will culminate in the creation of a group covenant like those created in the class meetings in early Methodism. Following the creation of the covenant, the group will remain together for two months, with members holding one another accountable to their mutually agreed-upon practices. Taken together, then, the three-month period will give participants a chance not only to learn but also to be molded through loving accountability into the people God has called

---

22. Thomas Oppong, "Psychological Secrets to Hack Your Way to Better Life Habits," *Observer*, March 20, 2017, https://observer.com/2017/03/psychological-secrets-hack-better-life-habits-psychology-productivity/.

23. My thanks to Scott A. Couchenour, founder of Serving Strong, www.servingstrong.com.

them to be. At the end of the three months, the group members will be invited to either remain in the covenant-based group or become group leaders themselves. Those who choose leadership will find a group of people to nurture in the same ways they have been nurtured.

While other group models exist and are widely used, none of them share the unique blend of accountability, sustainability, and multiplication that the covenant-based discipleship model offers. This model is designed with the end goal of fulfilling the Great Commission through the practices of holiness of heart and life. Finally, the covenant-based model will fit within the framework of most churches who typically offer Sunday school or small group options. This proposal is unique and will not be a duplication of existing models. For this reason, it may exist either alongside current local church offerings or as an alternative approach to discipleship. (See appendixes A and B for the specifics of the covenant-based discipleship model.)

None of us is likely to travel to the moon, but we can embark on a life-changing journey nonetheless. The call of Jesus to be his followers and make disciples marks the way forward for us as believers. Like the moon mission, we can't get there alone. We need each other, and we need loving accountability.

APPENDIX A
Teaching Methodology

The specific name for the methodology emerging from this book is the Covenant Formation Group (CFG). In his sermon "The Great Privilege of Those Born of God" Wesley says, "God does not continue to act upon the soul unless the soul re-acts upon God. . . . He first loves us and manifests himself unto us. . . . He will not continue to breathe into our soul unless our soul breathes toward him again; unless our love, and prayer, and thanksgiving return to him."[1]

Here is the rationale for Wesley and ultimately this book. The grace of God and human responsibility are not opposites but rather work together. God's grace and human response are what authentic Christianity looks like. The CFG model attempts to marry these two concepts in a practical expression of discipleship. If our churches hope to reverse the impact of

---

1. John Wesley, Sermon 19: "The Great Privilege of Those That Are Born of God," in *John Wesley's Sermons*, 191.

nominal Christianity on their parishioners and reinvigorate the pursuit of holiness of heart and life, they will need to recommit to this Wesleyan model of grace and response. Covenant Formation Groups are an essential step in the right direction.

To fail in this regard is to place our churches in a kind of parallel with Wesley's observations in 1763:

> I was more convinced than ever, that the preaching like an Apostle, without joining together those that are awakened, and training them up in the ways of God, is only begetting children for the murderer. How much preaching has there been for these twenty years all over Pembrokeshire! But no regular societies, no discipline, no order or connexion; and the consequence is, that nine in ten of the once-awakened are now faster asleep than ever.[2]

The failure to link doctrine with practice was bemoaned by Wesley then and echoes to this day. The CFG model attempts to do for postmodern churchgoers what the class meeting did for eighteenth-century Methodists.

The Teaching Component

I bought a new truck once. I had the chance to look over the equipment offered for the model I chose and select what I wanted. The basics were "standard equipment"; the extras were "optional equipment." My budget didn't allow for many of the "options," but I did select a few. I'm concerned that sometimes we treat discipleship as something separate from conversion,

---

2. Wesley, Journal entry for August 25, 1763, in *Works of John Wesley*, ed. Jackson, 3:144.

almost as a kind of add-on for the most pious. Nothing could be further from Jesus's teaching in the New Testament. Perhaps if we recovered Jesus's intentions, we might also recover a passion for discipleship.

There must be a teaching component to the CFG. Many churchgoers are unaware of the dramatic impact the forces of rival kingdoms are having on them and their church. Discipleship, then, is seen as a kind of "optional" discipline for those who are really serious about the Christian life. Nothing could be further from the scriptural or Wesleyan truth, but nevertheless, this notion is strong. There must be a reintroduction to the scriptural understanding of discipleship, and John Wesley's interpretation is the best approach for us. It is in both Wesley's theology and methodology that a solution to the church's discipleship dilemma becomes apparent. In particular, teaching around Wesley's means of grace will be a welcome return to a vital doctrine often neglected in our congregations and will open the door, through the prudential means of grace, to creative thinking and solutions to waning discipleship effectiveness. Unfortunately, churches have offered dozens of discipleship emphases over the years, most of which were program heavy and light on actual life change. Instruction around the CFG model will be refreshing and provide not only renewed understanding but also a practical and repeatable model for the days ahead. These reasons underlie the creation of the six-week instructional component of the model.

The Experiential Component

As stated above, teaching alone is not sufficient for life change. Wesley built the Methodists around the affirmation that belief must always connect to actions. In light of this, I'm suggesting an experiential component. Following the sixth week of training, the participants in the CFG will work together to create a covenant upon which they all agree to hold one another accountable. The covenant will undoubtedly reflect new insights from the weeks of training but may also nuance some older principles that have never been fully embodied by the members. Once the covenant is complete, the experiential portion of the CFG begins. Group members will meet, very much in the fashion of the class meeting, to watch over one another in loving accountability. Like the early Methodists, this simple practice will result in lasting life change for the participants.

The experiential component is essential because, as Wesley instinctively knew, practice repeated over time helps to habituate virtue. Not altogether unlike the countless hours invested in their craft by virtuosos or star athletes, the repeated practice of godliness under the loving accountability of others brings about holiness of heart and life. This reality helps to explain the relatively long, by local church programming standards, two-month period of the CFG. It simply takes time to learn new holy habits. Additionally, the experiential component of the CFG will help to break the isolationist tendencies of much of modern evangelicalism. The "me and Jesus" mindset of many Christians will initially chafe at the thought of loving accountability, but when the desire for holiness meets with the work of God's Spirit, loving accountability will reveal itself as the way forward.

Accountability is the missing link in the postmodern church, and without it, the church's future is bleak. In this light, it is also apparent that the input of others in an environment like a CFG will help to identify when growth is taking place. Often it requires the perspective of another to give one an unbiased assessment of growth. Finally, and most importantly, the CFG model offers built-in accountability. The uniqueness of this model is that it is not contingent upon the theological training of the leader but is instead firmly rooted in the mutually agreed-upon covenant. The covenant orders the session and provides the "curriculum" for each meeting.

The Covenant Formation Group is, then, the practical way toward the fulfillment of Jesus's Great Commission. The extravagant grace of God enables us to live in right relationship with God. His mission becomes our mandate even though it goes against the flow of postmodern culture. Thankfully, through the means of grace, Christians like us can experience God's blessing, and through the loving accountability of a Covenant Formation Group, we can see the transformation we long to see in ourselves and the world around us.

You may be thinking, "It can't really be that easy." I believe it is. Jesus invented the small group with his twelve disciples. They lived in moment-by-moment accountability with Jesus, and they were transformed from ordinary fishermen to leaders of a movement that altered both history and eternity. John Wesley picked up this methodology and not only impacted the church of his day but also changed the fate of a nation.

What the church has unintentionally let slip from its practice, our culture has rediscovered, with loving accountability transforming addiction, fitness, weight loss, and other challenges. The church can recover this lost practice and finally begin to accomplish what Jesus's death and resurrection made possible—the reconciliation of humanity to God through being and making Christlike disciples.

APPENDIX B
Covenant Formation Groups in Detail

Purpose

As those pursuing weight loss, physical fitness, or freedom from addiction have learned, accountability is the key to lasting change. The Covenant Formation Group (CFG) provides this accountability through members "watching over one another in love," a phrase coined by John Wesley. Wesley was driven to see Christians truly become disciples of Jesus Christ and discovered that accountability was essential to this end. Wesley engendered life transformation through the early Methodist class meetings. Covenant Formation Groups are a traditioned innovation of this eighteenth-century Methodist hallmark. By meeting together around a mutually agreed-upon covenant, the members of a CFG will experience real and lasting change in their own pursuit of Christlikeness.

Scope

The process for Covenant Formation Groups is divided into six weeks of training, followed by two months of experience. Once the three-month training and experience have concluded, members may choose to either remain in the group or prepare for leadership of their own group, leading others through the process they have just completed.

Importantly, this curriculum will require a special level of commitment from would-be participants. Wesley considered attendance at the class meeting to be mandatory. A wholehearted commitment to the CFG will be required for admittance. Participants will be encouraged to attend in person, but if they are unable temporarily, electronic options are encouraged. If a person simply cannot commit to the three-month schedule, that person should be encouraged to wait until her or his schedule is more conducive.

The Six-Week Training

Participants will be asked to meet for seventy-five minutes for each of the eight training sessions. Each session is designed to inspire participants to move from wanting to pursue holiness but not knowing where to begin to a Wesleyan-holiness methodology adapted from the methodology of John Wesley. Wesley saw demonstrable life change, and so will participants as they learn and practice covenant discipleship.

The six weeks are broken into the following sessions:

Week 1—The Reach of Grace: For God So Loved

Week 2—The Point of Grace: God's Mission and My Purpose

Week 3—The People of Grace: What Is a Disciple?

Week 4—Challenges to Grace: Why Is Discipleship So Difficult?

Week 5—The Means of Grace: Activating God's Grace for God's Mission

Week 6—The Practical Grace of a Covenant Group: Loving Accountability in Action

Session Format

Catching Up with Each Other (Relational Connection): The sessions will begin with a few moments of casual interaction as participants catch up on the week's activities. Learning to interact with fellow participants will strengthen relational connections and enhance interaction. (5 minutes)

Praying for One Another (Prayer): The group leader will then call the group together and lead in an opening time of prayer asking for God's help in learning and growing in holiness. (3 minutes)

Getting to Know One Another (Icebreaker Question): The group leader will ask a simple question designed to get the group interacting and to engage the general topic of the lesson. (5 minutes)

Discussion Questions: Each session will be supplemented by discussion questions designed to inspire peer-to-peer learning among the participants.

Weekly Practice: At the close of each session, participants will be invited to engage in a weekly practice specifically designed to reinforce the training received.

Application: The session will be closed with applications made to everyday life in a discussion format, followed by a closing prayer for God's help in living into all that was learned.

Daily Devotional: Each week the participants will be encouraged to spend time in Bible reading and prayer. This daily interaction with God will give the Spirit of God the chance to remind participants each day of their commitment to grow in grace.

Covenant Writing: The final session will invite the group members to write a covenant upon which they mutually agree to be used as the format for the ensuing three-month CFG experience.

The Covenant Writing Process

The concept of covenant discipleship was revived by David Lowes Watson for the United Methodist Church. In his book, *Covenant Discipleship: Christian Formation through Mutual Accountability*, he outlines the process of covenant writing. Where Dr. Watson has "traditioned" the general rules of the Methodists in his covenant groups, we have elected to work from the "Covenant of Christian Conduct" in the *Manual, Church of the Nazarene, 2017–2021* as a starting place for every CFG. Using paragraphs 28 through 28.4, the CFG covenant should be written using the following guidelines:

1. The covenant should represent the group's desire to pursue a "new and holy way of life."[1] This focus matches perfectly John Wesley's emphasis on holiness of heart and life.

---

1. *Manual, Church of the Nazarene, 2017–2021* (Kansas City: Nazarene Publishing House, 2017), paras. 28, 28.2.

2. The basis for this covenant should be the Holy Scriptures.[2]

3. The covenant should, with the help of the Holy Spirit, be careful to avoid all evil and embrace the good in accordance with 1 Thessalonians 5:21-22, which says, "Test them all; hold on to what is good, reject every kind of evil."[3]

Beyond this foundation, the covenant should fall within the following parameters:[4]

1. The covenant should represent the aspirations of the group members but also be a document of grace recognizing that only with the help of the Spirit will the participants be able to live into the covenant. Additionally, people are bound to have good and not so good weeks. Grace should be extended while encouraging the efforts to keep trying.

2. The covenant in and of itself is not magic. It is, rather, a means of grace in the tradition of the early Methodists. Participants should be reminded that God will use this means as they cooperate with God in response.

3. A brief preamble to the covenant should be written that grounds the covenant in the work of the Spirit and reminds the group weekly of their common goal.

---

2. Ibid., para. 28.1.

3. Ibid., para. 28.4.

4. Watson, *Covenant Discipleship*, 113-22. Dr. Watson's guidelines for covenant writing and implementation have been revised to fit the model's parameters.

4. The clauses of the covenant should be agreed upon by all as reasonably attainable on a weekly basis.

5. The number of clauses is not predetermined but should be set by the group members as they consider covering each of them in the allotted one-hour weekly meeting.

6. A conclusion to the covenant should be written to summarize again the group's dependence upon the help of God and the group members' support for one another.

7. The covenant should then be signed by every member and a copy given to each member to keep and refer to often as a reminder of her or his commitment to grow in holiness of heart and life.

The Two-Month Experience

Having completed the training and written a mutually agreed-upon covenant, the CFG experience will proceed as follows:

- First, group members will gather and spend five minutes in relational updates.
- The group leader will then call the group to order and pray.
- Next the group leader will go first and offer her or his assessment of living up to the agreed-upon covenant. This will take place as a group member is selected to ask about the group leader's successes or failures in living up to the covenant in a question-and-answer format. For example, "John, how did it go this week as you tried to live more simply?" Group members will be invited to offer helpful comments.

- The group then proceeds one after the other to go over each part of the agreed-upon covenant, assessing her or his successes and failures in living up to the covenant. The group leader will ask the questions of each member and facilitate any group comments.
- Once the members have all given their personal assessments, the group leader will summarize with observations and close the meeting in prayer.
- It is important that the meetings last no more than one hour so that participants may find it possible to work this gathering into their already busy lives.

Covenant language is the language of the Scriptures, both Old Testament and New Testament. Scholars believe that the Hebrew word for "covenant" is derived from an Assyrian word meaning "shackle" or "fetter."[5] In this light, the value of a covenant format is revealed. Participants in the CFG are binding themselves with both an unfailing God and a supportive community. This "vertical" and "horizontal" relationship is anchored in the Great Commandment, where Christians are directed to love God and neighbor, and in a cruciform life anchored in Jesus's cross, itself an expression of supreme love of God and humanity. The value of the CFG is that it is a daily reminder of the simplicity and power of the covenant with God and fellow participants. May God bless the Covenant Formation Group as a means of grace in the twenty-first-century church as God blessed the class meeting of the early Methodists.

---

5. Ibid., 113.